Dylan Thomas

UNDER MILK WOOD
A PLAY FOR VOICES

Edited by
WALFORD DAVIES
University of Wales, Aberystwyth

and

RALPH MAUD
Simon Fraser University, British Columbia

EVERYMAN
J. M. DENT • LONDON

Under Milk Wood first published 1954
Under Milk Wood first published in Everyman Paperbacks 1977
This definitive edition of *Under Milk Wood* first published 1995
Reprinted 1996, 1997

J.M. Dent
Orion Publishing Group
Orion House
5 Upper St Martin's Lane
London WC2H 9EA

Typeset by Selwood Systems Ltd, Midsomer Norton
Printed in Great Britain by
The Guernsey Press Co. Ltd, Guernsey, C.I.

British Library Cataloguing-in-Publication Data is available
upon request.

ISBN 0 460 87765 8

Everyman, I will go with thee,
and be thy guide

CONTENTS

NOTE ON THE AUTHOR AND EDITORS

DYLAN MARLAIS THOMAS was born in Swansea on 27 October 1914. After leaving school he worked briefly as a junior reporter on the *South Wales Evening Post* before embarking on a literary career in London. There he rapidly established himself as one of the finest poets of his generation. *18 Poems* appeared in 1934, *Twenty-five Poems* in 1936, *The Map of Love* in 1939 and *Deaths and Entrances* in 1946; his *Collected Poems* was published in 1952. Throughout his life Thomas also wrote short stories, his most famous collection being *Portrait of the Artist as a Young Dog* (1940). He also wrote filmscripts, broadcast features and talks, lectured in America, and wrote the radio play *Under Milk Wood*. On 9 November 1953, shortly after his thirty-ninth birthday, he collapsed and died in New York. His body is buried in Laugharne, Wales, his home for many years.

WALFORD DAVIES is Director of the Department of Extra-Mural Studies at the University of Wales, Aberystwyth, where he also holds a personal chair in English Literature. His previous work on Dylan Thomas includes two studies of the poet, *Dylan Thomas* (1972) and *Dylan Thomas* (1986), and the following editions published by J. M. Dent: *Early Prose Writings* (1971), *New Critical Essays* (1972) and *Selected Poems* (1993). His edition of *Deaths and Entrances* appeared in 1984, and other publications include editions of the poetry of Wordsworth, Gerard Manley Hopkins and Thomas Hardy.

RALPH MAUD is Professor of English at Simon Fraser University, British Columbia. Among his previous works on Dylan Thomas are *Entrances to Dylan Thomas's Poetry* (1963), and the following editions: *The Colour of Saying: an Anthology of Verse Spoken by Dylan Thomas* (with Aneirin Talfan Davies, Dent, 1963), *The Notebook Poems* (Dent, 1989), and *Wales in his Arms: Dylan Thomas's Choice of Welsh Poetry* (1994). His *Dylan Thomas in Print* (Dent, 1972) is the standard bibliography. Walford Davies and Ralph Maud are also the joint editors of *Dylan Thomas: Collected Poems 1934-1953* (Dent, 1988).

BRIEF CHRONOLOGY

27 Oct 1914	Dylan Marlais Thomas born in Swansea
Sept 1925	Enters Swansea Grammar School, where his father was Senior English Master
27 Apr 1930	Starts the first of the 'Notebooks' into which he copied his early poems. (The Notebooks continued until Apr 1934)
Aug 1931	Leaves school. Employed as Reporter on the *South Wales Evening Post* (until Dec 1932)
Mar 1933	First poem published in London ('And death shall have no dominion' in the *New English Weekly*)
Aug 1933	First visit to London
Sept 1933	First poem published in 'Poet's Corner' of the *Sunday Referee* ('That Sanity be Kept'). Correspondence with Pamela Hansford Johnson begins
22 Apr 1934	Wins Book Prize of the 'Poet's Corner' – i.e., the *Sunday Referee*'s sponsorship of his first collection of poems
Feb–Nov 1934	Several visits to London
10 Nov 1934	Moves to live in London
18 Dec 1934	*18 Poems* published
Apr 1936	Meets Caitlin Macnamara
10 Sept 1936	*Twenty-five Poems* published
21 Apr 1937	First radio broadcast ('Life and the Modern Poet')
11 Jul 1937	Marries Caitlin Macnamara
May 1938	First moved to live in Laugharne, Carmarthenshire

30 Jan 1939	First son (Llewelyn) born, in Hampshire
24 Aug 1939	*The Map of Love* (poems and stories) published
20 Dec 1939	*The World I Breathe* (a selection of his poetry and prose) – his first volume publication in America
4 Apr 1940	*Portrait of the Artist as a Young Dog* (short stories) published
July 1940	Leaves Laugharne for London
Sept 1940	Begins work as script-writer for films with the Strand Film Company
1940–2	Living partly in London, partly in Wales
Late 1942	Brings wife and son to live in Chelsea
Feb 1943	*New Poems* (USA)
3 Mar 1943	Daughter (Aeronwy) born
1943	Continuous work as broadcaster begins
Sept 1944 –summer 1945	Living at New Quay, Cardiganshire
Summer 1945 –spring 1946	Living in London
7 Feb 1946	*Deaths and Entrances* published
Mar 1946 –May 1949	Living in or near Oxford
8 Nov 1946	*Selected Writings* (USA)
Apr–Aug 1947	Visits Italy
Sept 1947	Moves to live in South Leigh, Oxfordshire
1948	Writing feature films for Gainsborough
Mar 1949	Visits Prague as guest of Czechoslovak government
May 1949	Laugharne again becomes his main home (The Boat House)
24 Jul 1949	Second son (Colm) born

Feb–Jun 1950	First American tour
Jan 1951	In Iran, writing film script for the Anglo Iranian Oil Company
Jan–May 1952	Second American tour
Feb 1952	*In Country Sleep* (USA)
10 Nov 1952	*Collected Poems 1934–1952* published
16 Dec 1952	The poet's father dies
31 Mar 1953	*Collected Poems* (USA)
Apr–Jun 1953	Third American tour
14 May 1953	First performance of *Under Milk Wood* in New York
14 May 1953	*The Doctor and the Devils*. The first of the film scripts to be published
Oct 1953	Leaves on final American tour
9 Nov 1953	Dies in St Vincent's Hospital, New York City

INTRODUCTION
The Road to Milk Wood

I

During his last days in New York City in November 1953, while making cuts in the script of *Under Milk Wood* for its appearance in the stylish American periodical *Mademoiselle*, Dylan Thomas told Elizabeth Reitell that he looked forward to the time when he could prepare a 'literary version for trade publication'.[1] Three years earlier he had made the same point in a letter to Marguerite Caetani: 'Now, I am writing a long radio play, which will, I am sure, come to life on the printed page as well'.[2] The poet's untimely death left us with an *Under Milk Wood* cast strictly as a radio play commissioned by the BBC, and broadcast posthumously as such on 25 January 1954. In the same year, it was the broadcast script that was presented to the reading public under the editorship of Daniel Jones, with the subtitle 'A Play for Voices'. As the present editors proceeded with the task of examining Thomas's manuscripts of the play in order to confirm or adjust the previously standard Jones text, they could not help hearing the poet's references to a 'literary version' as a plea to be acted upon.

Accordingly, the present edition is designed to be a more readable version of the play for the printed page. It became clear that the purpose of the division of the narration into a First Voice and a Second Voice was to alleviate the burden on the actors taking those parts and to achieve limited effects of variation through the different timbre of their voices. In a broadcast or a stage performance the audience might get some benefit from this device. But readers of the published Jones edition of *Under Milk Wood* are, by the very existence of this split in the narration, handed a problem – that of having to read the words 'First Voice' precisely 110 times and the words 'Second Voice' precisely 77 times. It is not as if Thomas had made the First and Second Voices distinguishable through traits of speech patterns, imagery, personality, or depth of soul.[3] By relieving the reader of the 187 switches that the eye had formerly to pay attention to, the present edition frees the reading ear to hear what is in reality one narrative guide to the action of the play. It should also be noted that when the original BBC producer, Douglas Cleverdon, came to prepare an Acting Version for J. M. Dent in 1958 he decided on one narrator.

Thomas actually began the play with the idea of a single narrator. When John Malcolm Brinnin visited Laugharne in the summer of 1951 and Thomas read him parts of what was then called 'Llareggub Hill', the work was to consist of 'an interweaving of many voices', but 'with the strong central voice of a narrator to supply the unities of time, place, and situation'.[4] When Thomas had finished about half the play, he sent it for publication to the Italian journal *Botteghe Oscure* in October 1951, and wrote about it in a letter to the editor, Marguerite Caetani: 'As the piece goes on, two voices will be predominant: that of the preacher, who talks only in verse, and that of the anonymous exhibitor and chronicler called, simply, 1st Voice' (*Collected Letters*, 814). Even though the Second Voice was already in this 'piece for radio perhaps' that he was offering to *Botteghe Oscure*, Thomas chose to speak only of the First Voice, as of a single narrator: 'the 1st Voice is really a kind of conscience, a guardian angel. Through him you will learn about Mr. Edwards, the draper, and Miss Price, the sempstress', and so on. Thomas ends his description by saying: 'the 1st Voice, and the poet preacher, never judge nor condemn but explain and make strangely simple and simply strange'. The play confirms what we can here deduce from the poet's own words: that there is really no separate role for the Second Voice in the action or the significance of the work . This edition therefore employs a single-voice italicised narration as a format better suited to introduce, and lead us into and through, the various delights of the play.

2

Those delights were long in the making. Like all works that mark the end of a career, *Under Milk Wood* has a classic status as the expression of a late vision of life. And like that of so many artists, Thomas's late vision is a celebratory one, in which ripeness is all. But, like Chaucer in the General Prologue to the *Canterbury Tales*, Thomas is as intelligent about the gravity underlying comic celebration as about comic celebration itself. In describing *Under Milk Wood*'s wonderful comedy, our language often needs to be dual, to fall between light and shade, like Raymond Williams's description of the play as Thomas's 'adequate epilogue, his uproarious and singing lament'.[5] We have to remember that the play's period of gestation was Thomas's whole career, and that the hinterland of poetry, prose, film and broadcasts from which the play emerged was often a dark one. In outlining the growth of the idea of writing the play itself, therefore, it will be useful to bear in mind this wider relationship to the rest of the career.

Under Milk Wood is twenty-four hours in the life of a small Welsh seaside town. That basic idea went back as far as 1932 when Thomas and his Swansea friend Bert Trick began formulating very loosely a plan to write a Welsh *Ulysses*.[6] In 1932, the relevance of James Joyce lay only in the use of a twenty-four hour cycle in the town's life. But the Irishman's influence survived at a more important level twenty years later in the actual writing of the play. Apart from Joycean puns and verbal inventiveness in general, there is in *Under Milk Wood* the particular influence of the Circe nighttown episode in *Ulysses*, itself a kind of 'play for voices'. Most obvious is the crisp usefulness Thomas remembered from the way in which Joyce projected his speakers first of all through the filter of a narrator's description:

> BLOOM: (Barefoot, pigeonbreasted, in lascar's vest and trousers, apologetic toes turned in, opens his tiny mole's eyes and looks about him dazedly, passing a slow hand across his forehead. Then he hitches his belt sailor fashion and with a shrug of oriental obeisance salutes the court, pointing one thumb heavenward...)

The sheer frequency of this formula in the nighttown episode of *Ulysses* made it memorable, but of course Thomas made his own, endlessly inventive use of it:

> Mister Waldo, rabbitcatcher, barber, herbalist, catdoctor, quack, his fat, pink hands, palms up, over the edge of the patchwork quilt, his black boots neat and tidy in the washing basin, his bowler on a nail above the bed... (p. 8)

No wonder that in a High Court case in 1966 to settle a dispute regarding the ownership of the play's original manuscript, one of the parties took the oath describing himself as 'bookseller, writer, publisher, editor, extra-mural tutor, lecturer, wigmaker and examiner in Hairdressing for the City and Guilds'.[7] *Under Milk Wood* had obviously made a mark by making such flourishes very much its own.

A writer open to stylistic models of this kind, and in search of material, could have found plenty of colour and character in Thomas's native Swansea, which he once described as 'marble-town, city of laughter, little Dublin' (*Collected Letters*, 435) and where certainly *Under Milk Wood*'s satire on bourgeois hypocrisy first took root. But his Swansea experiences found their appropriate, and still Joycean, form in the autobiographical short stories of *Portrait of the Artist as a Young Dog* (1940), which were written in 1938 and 1939. In moving to live in Laugharne in Carmarthenshire in 1938, a village he had first visited with Glyn Jones in 1934, thinking it even then 'the strangest town in Wales' (*Collected Letters*, 135), the poet found another, more encompassable, community that kept shady eccentricity and idyllic atmosphere in optimum balance. Laugharne's character stemmed from its position between two cultures which was the result of its Teutonic settlement in the twelfth century when English displaced Welsh, but without obliterating its signatures – its dialect and place-names, for example. The village's odd separateness was a subject in a major *History of Carmarthenshire* published at this time, in which T. Gwynn Jones wrote of Laugharne:

> The outlook of the people through the centuries was seaward. Their maritime activities established contacts for the purposes of trade and commerce with English and foreign ports. Such an intercourse must have had its influence on the life of this foreign colony, though it does not appear to have produced at any period a strong stimulus to mental or spiritual awakening. Intellectually and culturally, these settlements remained largely in isolation, whilst their life was separated from that of the neighbouring Welsh by an artificial boundary, resulting from a deep consciousness of wide national differences.[8]

But Thomas immediately recognised Laugharne's uniqueness for himself. While predictably relishing the local colour ('It's a sociable place too, and I like that, with good pubs and little law and no respect', *Collected Letters*, 294), he also divined, with rare instinct, the underlying source of Laugharne's precise chemistry: 'The people speak with a broad English accent, although on all sides they are surrounded by hundreds of miles of Welsh county. The neutral sea lies at the foot of the town' (*Collected Letters*, 135).

It took many years for these impressions to mature artistically, but even in 1939 he recognised their literary potential. In December that year, at a 'Laugharne Entertainment' organised in aid of the Red Cross, Dylan Thomas, Frances Hughes (wife of the novelist Richard Hughes) and Mr Gleed the local butcher took the leading parts in Ernest Goodwin's one-act farce, *The Devil Among the Skins*. 'What Laugharne really needs,' Thomas told Richard Hughes and the others afterwards, 'is a play about well-known Laugharne characters – and get them all to play themselves'.[9] It is an interesting concept. At its first night in 1634, Milton's *Comus* had the advantage of having the children whom the masque was designed to praise play themselves. At the other end of the social spectrum, and in such different times, one cannot any longer imagine a work of universal appeal arising from such total, local fusion of acted and actor. And yet there was something oddly prophetic about it. During the war years that followed, several patriotic films celebrating the role of small communities in withstanding German might – the Welsh community of *The Silent Village* (1943), for example – had the villagers playing themselves. Even in the first broadcast of *Under Milk Wood* on the brand-new Third Programme of the BBC in January 1954 it was considered crucial that the playful singing children should be the actual children of Laugharne. And in 1988, producers of the star-studded EMI recording decided that even the actual silences and bell-notes of Laugharne – what their sound-recordists called the 'ambience' of Laugharne – should 'play themselves'. This general feel of uniqueness, of a sweet *especial* rural scene, is a clear tribute to place and play alike. It is in that context that the particular contribution of Laugharne's inhabitants remains important. *Under Milk Wood* is not a *roman à clef*, but models for a good number of its eccentrics must have been available early for Thomas to have made that point to Richard Hughes about the possibility of villagers playing themselves. On this central importance of Laugharne, Caitlin Thomas's first-hand testimony is unequivocal:

> Dylan loved all that small-town pomp and the nonsense gossip that he lapped up every morning in Ivy Williams' kitchen at Brown's Hotel ... Dylan found it very cosy, and it was there that he picked up all the character vignettes which he moulded into *Under Milk Wood*. The folk of Laugharne were engaged in an endless wrangle of feuds, affairs, fights, frauds and practical jokes ... Dylan captured all that, and the lives of the more respectable people behind their blinds who wouldn't come to the pub anyway, who wore their best Sunday suits, and walked to church with a Bible under their arms: he saw it all.[10]

Part of the authentic gusto of the play, its feel for the atmosphere and detail of a small town – the cobbles and sea-fry as well as the human foibles – came from the fact that its material wasn't completely invented. The place which gave it a local habitation and a name was already strange enough.

Probably the idea of a Laugharne play occurred to Thomas at just that time because of an invitation from the Welsh novelist T. Rowland

Hughes, then a BBC Welsh Region producer in Cardiff, to contribute to a plan 'to develop Verse Features, that is, long dramatic programmes in verse'.[11] Thomas showed interest, but doubted his talent in that direction: 'I take such a long time writing anything, and the result, dramatically, is too often like a man shouting under the sea' (*Collected Letters*, 337). But the detailed vividness of Laugharnian material would have struck him as just the stuff to compensate for the absence of any more orthodox 'dramatic' powers. At the same time, we should remember that 1938 was very much a transitional year for Thomas, in which his art was already changing direction. A poem of that year, 'After the funeral (In Memory of Ann Jones)', shows him turning outwards to a more varied Welsh world. The need to develop towards more objective material came from a feeling of deadlock in his writing of poetry, and the 1938 poem 'On no work of words', in notebook lines later discarded, associated the feeling with the easy-going indolence of Laugharne itself:

> For three lean months now, no work done
> In summer Laugharne among the cockle boats
> And by the castle with the boatlike birds.[12]

At the same time, 1938 was the year in which Thomas started energetically writing the ten short stories that were to comprise *Portrait of the Artist as a Young Dog*, published in 1940. It was these stories above all else that started training the vivid comic eye that later made *Under Milk Wood* possible.

The Second World War had its own sinister contribution to make. As early as 1934 Thomas had volunteered the proposition that 'artists, as far as I can gather, have set out, however unconsciously, to prove one of two things: either that they are mad in a sane world, or that they are sane in a mad world' (*Collected Letters*, 90). In 1943 Thomas outlined (again to Richard Hughes) an idea that shows that his need to start thinking of a structure for his play was taking him in some strange directions. A whole village is certified as mad by an Inspector sent down from London, and this despite the fact that, as the villagers' own testimony proves, they are a veritable island of sanity in a mad world. A year or so later, Thomas developed the idea further in conversation with Constantine FitzGibbon. The village was now to be declared not only mad but dangerous: 'Barbed wire was strung about it and patrolled by sentries, lest its dotty inhabitants infect the rest of the world'.[13] FitzGibbon makes it clear that Thomas now had in mind not only the mad world of arbitrary detention and POW camps but also the obscenity of the Nazi concentration camps, by then nightmare reality, not mere rumour.

What made further thought about such plans worthwhile was the sudden burgeoning of Thomas's career as a radio broadcaster. He had been reading poetry and acting on radio on an occasional basis since 1939. But from 1943 onwards the frequency of his contributions grew enormously. If we include readings, in the ten years left to him he was to record no fewer than 156 broadcasts or contributions to broadcasts – of which, most importantly, 28 were creative scripts of his own. The script most relevant to our story at this point is 'Quite Early One Morning', a radio feature recorded for the Welsh Home Service in December 1944, and the first attempt at portraying a sleeping community, the very basis of *Under Milk Wood*. 'Quite Early One Morning' sprang from Thomas's experience of living, between September 1944 and July 1945, at New Quay, a seaside village on the Cardiganshire coast. The broadcast portrays the still-sleeping community and its dreams as a visitor moves through its streets on an early morning in winter, 'like a stranger come out of the sea'.[14] At the end, prototypes for characters such as Captain Cat, Eli Jenkins and Mrs Ogmore-Pritchard speak in quatrains. The narrator, however, is as good as being Thomas himself, the idiom of the work being essentially that of a short story or essay. But New Quay, so similar in many ways to Laugharne, was crucial in supplementing the gallery of characters Thomas had to hand for writing *Under Milk Wood*. New Quay's role as an extra source is also clear from letters. An August 1946 letter to Margaret Taylor, for example, who visited New Quay a year after the Thomases' period there:

> I wish New Quay had had more sun for you, though Jack Pat loves it as it is for then he has his guests all trapped and cosy in his godly grot. Time has stopped, says the Black Lion clock, and Eternity has begun. I'm so glad you met and like Dai Fred who bottled your ship. Did you come across Dewi, the battery-man? Evan Joshua of the Bluebell? The Norman you know is New Quay's noisiest and least successful fighter; every summer he starts a fight, and every summer some tiny little ape-man knocks him yards over the harbour-wall or bang through the chemist's window. Did Mrs Evans the Lion twitch, wink, and sip? Did Pat bring his horse in the bar? Jack the Post is an old friend: he once married a pretty widow in London and everything was fine, he said, except that wherever they went they were followed by men in bowler hats. After the honeymoon, Mrs Jack was arrested for double bigamy. And all the husbands appeared

in the court and gave evidence as to her good character ... Did you meet Taffy Jones, the stuttering ace? He's not very nice. Or Alistair Graham, the thin-vowelled laird? (*Collected Letters*, 603)

'Quite Early One Morning' was too short a piece in which to exercise the 'mad town' idea in any structured way, but the idea seems hinted at in embryo in a joke regarding one unpopular inhabitant of the village of that 1944 broadcast, a 'retired male nurse who had come to live in Wales after many years' successful wrestling with the mad rich of Southern England':

> He measured you for a strait-jacket carefully with his eye; he saw you bounce from rubber walls like a sorbo ball. No behaviour surprised him. Many people of the town found it hard to resist leering at him suddenly around the corner, or convulsively dancing, or pointing with laughter and devilish good humour at invisible dog-fights merely to prove to him that they were normal. (*Broadcasts*, 13)

More importantly, 'Quite Early One Morning' was a veritable storehouse of phrases, rhythms and details later resurrected or modified for *Under Milk Wood*: 'deeper waves than ever tossed', 'bombazine-black', 'the knitted text and the done-by-hand watercolours', and the 'big seas of dreams'. The success of the broadcast prompted Thomas to discuss with friends whether any extension of the basic material should take the form of a stage comedy in verse or a radio play whose central character was a blind narrator. That last point in particular shows that we are definitely on the road to Captain Cat's Milk Wood.

There are other milestones on the road, to which we shall return. At this point it is worth leaping ahead to late 1950 when Thomas decided that the 'Town That Was Mad' idea (now seen as a potential radio play for the BBC) was, in that form, a false destination. In this respect, a thirty-nine page holograph fair-copy of roughly the first half of the play, now at Texas, is crucial. It is a manuscript abandoned at exactly the point at which Thomas had started actually to implement the 'Town That Was Mad' scenario. Up to that point, the manuscript was completely in the manner of the play as we now know it, without a hint of any stricter 'plot' of any kind. After some changes and rearrangements, it was the text sent to *Botteghe Oscure* in October 1951 and published there as 'Llareggub, A Piece for Radio Perhaps' in April 1952. That material ended with Captain Cat listening to the gossiping women ('who's dead, who's dying, the cost of soapflakes ...') and joining in the children's chanting against the background of chapel organ music – the kind of stuff we now normally associate with the play. But in the manuscript this led into the following, very different scene:

> *Noise of Powerful Motor-Car Roars into*
> *Organ-Music. Car pulls up near.*

Captain Cat (Softly, to himself)

> Foreigners!
> A nasty, powerful, new motor.
> What's it doing here?
>   *Hum and babble of voices near, Organ in background.*

1st Voice

> Blow the horn, Freddie . . .

2nd Voice

> Scratch your name on the mudguard, Freddie . . .

3rd Voice

> The man in the bowler's getting out . . .

1st Voice

> Now you can blow the horn, Freddie . . .

Official

> Where does Captain Tudor live?

3rd Voice

> He doesn't live here . . .

4th Voice

> We got no Captain Tudor . . .

2nd Voice

> Captain Cat's the only Captain.

3rd Voice

> And *he's* blind.

4th Voice

> We call him Captain Cat because he can see in the dark.

Captain Cat (loudly)

> Who wants me?

Official

> Are you Captain Tudor?

Captain Cat

> I was.

Official Letter [sic]

> I am to deliver an *important* sealed letter to you personally.

Captain Cat

> Bring it up the gangway then.

Noise of Feet on Cobbles
Loud Note on Motor Horn

1st Voice

Good old Freddie.

Captain Cat

What's the letter?

Official

My instructions are to deliver it to you without comment or explanation.

Captain Cat

Put it in my good hand then. The one with four fingers.

Noise of Car Driving Off
Organ Music

Captain Cat (softly, to himself)

Letters with seals from men with voices like puddings are important. I must call a meeting.

Feet Crossing Room
Noise of Ship's Hooter
The Organ Music finishes on an unresolved chord.

Fade Out
Fade In
Murmur of Voices Outside in Background
One Knock on Door

Captain Cat

Come in, Organ Morgan.

Two Knocks

Captain Cat

Come in, Mr Pugh.

Three Knocks

Captain Cat

Come in, Mr Eli Jenkins.

This scene, abandoned at that point, proves that the manuscript is the one that Thomas sent to Douglas Cleverdon, radio producer at the BBC, in late 1950, calling it 'the first thirty-nine pages of the provisionally titled "The Town That Was Mad"' (*Collected Letters*, 773). Also at Texas are eight pages of Savage Club notepaper – numbered 40–47, clearly to lead on from this thirty-nine page manuscript – on which Thomas describes the turn that the play was now going to take. The 'Town That Was Mad' idea has been so often paraphrased at several removes by friends who remembered Thomas describing it that it is useful to have it for once in Thomas's own words:

Now follows a scene between Captain Cat, Eli Jenkins, Organ Morgan, and Mr Pugh. Captain Cat asks Eli Jenkins if he will read aloud the important letter which has just arrived. Eli Jenkins, finding that the letter is not in verse, confesses his inability to do so. Organ Morgan can, of course, read only music. Captain Cat is blind. And so Mr Pugh has to read the letter. It is a statement from the department of the New Government of Wales. The statement says, in effect: There appears to be no reason why this town should not be declared an Insane Area. As it is not expedient to commit the whole population of the town to a lunatic asylum, we now declare this town itself to be a lunatic asylum. It will be cordoned off as such. Traffic that used to pass through it will be diverted. No goods will be allowed to come into it. The asylum must live upon the fish it can get from the sea and the crops it can get from the land. It is the intention of the Government to allow this town to fall redundant. Etc etc etc.

There is consternation in Captain Cat's cabin. This lovely town of theirs an Insane Area? The idea is preposterous. The place is, as much as any place can be, sane and happy. Captain Cat decides that the town must know immediately the terrible slur that has been cast upon it. And Eli Jenkins, Organ Morgan, and Mr Pugh rush out to spread the news. Captain Cat, after hooting the siren, goes out to pull the townhall bell. The school bell also rings. Clocks chime. The organ plays. We hear snatches of startled talk, indignation, and conjecture from all over the town as the inhabitants hurry to meet in the Town Hall Square. There, Captain Cat addresses them from his window. He tells them the great insulting news. There is a pandemonium of protest. *We are not mad*, cry the people of the town. And, after the turbulent meeting, Cat, Jenkins, Morgan and Pugh draft a letter to the Government denying the town's insanity and insisting that the town's defence of its sanity be heard.

A Trial is arranged, a Trial in which the defendant is the sanity of the whole community.

The Trial is held in the Town Hall. The Government has sent down an official prosecution. The town's defending counsel is Captain Cat. The witnesses are the people of the town.

One by one the principal inhabitants of the town step forward (these are the characters whom we have already briefly met) and give evidence. The Government Prosecution details the eccentricity of each witness. The witness[es], admitting the facts, deny they prove eccentricity. And Captain

Cat shows how each case of eccentricity, or near-madness, is, in reality, only an [in]stance of the right of the individual to lead his own life in his own way. Relentlessly, the Prosecution shows up the insanity of each individual witness. And relentlessly, but with fun and feeling, Captain Cat defends, approves, and even, sometimes, glorifies it. The Prosecution sums up. He posits an ideally sane town. By its standards, *this* town is mad as a hatter.

Captain Cat sums up. He decries the ideal town, but says that, by its standards, this town is, indeed, insane. And thank God for it.

With the approval of the whole population, Captain Cat accepts the Government's jurisdiction. Yes, we are mad, he says. This town is mad. We are content to be so. Cordon us off. Declare us an Insane Area. We will continue to live as long as we can, alone, a community of individual people.

If any further parts of this scheme were actually written, they do not seem to have survived. Some friends (Vernon Watkins, for example) seemed to remember Thomas 'quoting' such parts, but these were probably memories of Thomas vividly paraphrasing or improvising potential ideas. Douglas Cleverdon, eagerly waiting for the long-protracted work to arrive in any final form at all, recalls Thomas's relief when he suggested, in late 1950, that the only way ahead was to drop the 'Mad Town' plot altogether.[15] Though Thomas told Marguerite Caetani that he did so reluctantly and only temporarily, and though one of the play's best critics, Raymond Williams, regrets the abandonment of the plot, it was in more ways than one a sound decision on Thomas's part. The transitional section quoted above has one or two things that might be effective in a radio medium. The car noise breaking harshly into the children's chanting, for example, and leaving the organ music on 'an unresolved chord', reminds us suddenly of an outside world. It makes us realise for the first time how unrealistically absorbed we have been in this precarious 'place of love' (p. 56), as if it were itself the whole world. It works like a pale version of the Knocking at the Gate in *Macbeth* – with the negative world being this time the intruder. But the functionalism of this more direct 'drama' was clearly uncongenial to Thomas. That much is clear in the hopelessly attenuated verbal texture that the suddenly implemented 'plot' now called for ('The man in the bowler's getting out', and so on). In the outline of the remainder of the plot even the nature of the comedy changes: in Eli Jenkins's inability to read anything but verse, or Organ Morgan's to read anything but music, eccentricity is in danger of crossing over into idiocy.

This is no permanent criticism. These are manuscripts and outlines. Thomas would have recognised and largely mitigated their dangers. But he decided instead not to continue on that road at all. He knew better than anyone that his strengths did not lie in extended 'plots' of any kind. The only firm frameworks that were ever congenial to him were the intricate verse-forms of his poetry. In all other respects his genius was essentially lyrical, capitalising on the vividness of parts within loose structures. His early scheme for a 'novel of the Jarvis Valley', for example, was planned only as a collection of short stories with a common setting; his prose works regularly took advantage of the simple framework of events over the course of one day; his nearest attempt at autobiography, *Portrait of the Artist as a Young Dog*, again took the form of short stories; and arguably his most ambitious poem, 'Altarwise by owl-light', is significantly a sonnet sequence. In the same way, his late poetic masterwork was to be 'In Country Heaven', only sixteen lines of whose frame was finished, and whose contents were mainly individual poems already completed. In the case of the play, Thomas, always conscientious in this respect, had probably thought that a contract for a sixty- or ninety-minute script made an orthodox plot compulsory. But given the kind of writer he was, any 'structure', grafted onto more congenial parts, always ran the risk of tissue rejection.

3

The problem was solved when the job in hand was seen as a radio 'feature' not as a radio play. Douglas Cleverdon has crystallised the distinction:

> A radio play is a dramatic work deriving from the tradition of the theatre, but conceived in terms of radio. A radio feature is, roughly, any constructed programme (that is, other than news bulletins, racing commentaries, and so forth) that derives from the technical apparatus of radio ... It can combine any sound elements – words, music, sound effects – in any form or mixture of forms – documentary, actuality, dramatised, poetic, musico-dramatic. It has no rules determining what can or cannot be done. And though it may be in dramatic form, it has no need of a dramatic plot. (*Cleverdon*, 17)

Thomas was at home with the idea of the 'radio feature' as the proper form. He had already done several of them, most significantly

'The Londoner', broadcast in 1946. Springing from an aborted idea
for a book about the streets of London that had planned 'to take the
life of the streets from twelve noon to twelve midnight' (*Collected
Letters*, 537), 'The Londoner' in fact covers a twenty-four-hour span
in the lives of an ordinary post-war London family of four. It opens
and closes with night and dreams. The big step forward from 'Quite
Early One Morning' came in activating a greater number of characters, sympathetically compèred by an omniscient Narrator. Even while
fulfilling the sociological aim of the documentary series in which it
figured (*This is London*, for the Overseas Service), 'The Londoner'
makes room for a good deal of comic effect, much more than would
have been allowed to another writer. *Under Milk Wood*'s use of
gossiping women, of low-keyed poetry, of interrupted or mis-
understood dialogues are all here in embryo, along with the basic
effect of fantasy:

> NARRATOR: It's nearly half past six on a summer morning. Montrose
> Street is awake.
>
> [Noise of Cars and Lorries]
>
> NARRATOR: But most of the houses are still sleeping. In number 49, all
> is quiet. Lily Jackson is dreaming.
>
> [Music]
>
> LILY: Ooh, what a beautiful dress ... like the one Ingrid Bergman was
> wearing in what-was-the name ... And the music! Lovelier than oh-I-
> can't-remember, the one with the violin and the big sad eyes. Look,
> they're walking down the aisle, white as Christmas. There's lights all
> over the place like victory night. Oh, it's all changing. They're dancing
> in a kind of palace now ... Look, there's Mrs Cooley next door with a
> dustcap on ... They're singing ... I'm there too ... I'm dancing on the
> falling snow ... Where's Ted ... where's Ted? (*Broadcasts*, 77)

Praise for 'The Londoner' by Laurence Gilliam, BBC Head of
Features, led to an invitation to write another feature immediately.
The result was 'Margate – Past and Present' (1946), recorded for
transmission on a New York station in exchange for an American
feature on New York's Coney Island. Again the structure is simply
the passage of one day, though not from dreaming night to dreaming
night. Framing the piece, rather too much like book-ends, are two
exchanges between a First Voice and a Second Voice, who have no
part at all to play in the body of the piece itself. The aim is essentially
documentary – an evocation of Margate being considered a fair
exchange for one of Coney Island, and a good focus for a view of

post-war British life. Thomas makes intelligent, inventive use of a return visit by an American ex-serviceman from Coney Island to marry the English girl he left behind a year before. But the dialogue shows the strain of having to fulfil also the function of description and narrative – as when the American tells his girlfriend 'See this giggle of girls coming towards us with cellophane hats? "Kiss Me Quick" "I'll Have to Ask Me Dad" "I'm no Angel" ...' (*Broadcasts*, 108).

A more desperate contingency in that respect was the introduction of the Voice of an Information Book about Margate, communicating the raw details of its population, tourist industry and history. This particular device however is in a lineage of some relevance to *Under Milk Wood*. In 'The Town That Was Mad' the accusation against the community was very much that of outsiders. In 'Quite Early One Morning' there was the male nurse (a newcomer) who wanted the villagers to appear madder than they were. In 'The Londoner' the 'Voice of an Expert' prompted a more realistic insight into this gap between outside perception and inner reality:

QUESTIONER: And what is Montrose Street? What does it look like?
VOICE OF AN EXPERT: It is a grey-bricked street of one hundred houses. Built in 1890. Two bedrooms, a front room and a kitchen. Bathrooms were built into less than half of the houses in 1912. A scullery and a backyard. Rent 28 shillings. Too cold in the winter, too hot in the summer. Ugly, inconvenient, and infinitely depressing.
VOICE OF AN OLD RESIDENT: No, no. You got it all wrong. It's a nice, lively street. There's all the shops you want at one end, and there's pubs at both ends. Mightn't be much to look at, but there's always things going on, there's always something to see, buses and trams and lorries and prams and kids and dogs and dogfights sometimes and ... (*Broadcasts*, 76)

The Old Resident's objection is of the kind so tragically ignored by those 'experts' who soon afterwards were building the high-rise blocks of our inner cities. The reduction of a community to statistics by outsiders who think only in cold orthodoxies is a vestige of the 'Town That Was Mad' scenario. Along with Captain Cat's plea for a 'community of individual people', it reminds us that Thomas had shared the 1930s with the Auden group, and shared Auden's focus on the 'average man ... put through the statistician's hoop' ('New Year Letter') or the 'Unknown Citizen' who 'was found by the bureau of statistics to be/One against whom there was no official complaint'.

Thomas's broadcasts are at the post-war, small-time, domestic end of a current of feeling that in the poetry of the 1930s produced 'heroic' anti-totalitarian allegories, a current still live in Orwell's anti-Stalinist *Animal Farm* (1945) and anti-political *Nineteen Eighty-four* (1949). The socialist credentials (or public-school confidence) of it all are not to be looked for in the Welsh fantasy of *Under Milk Wood*, but there is in the play an authentic 'popular' commitment that is not unrelated. Even the outsider impersonality of 'Voice of an Expert' and 'Voice of Information' survives in the play – in the Voice of a Guidebook, a softer parody of a softer target, but still an exquisite thrust at patronisation of the regions:

> Less than five hundred souls inhabit the three quaint streets and the few narrow bylanes and scattered farmsteads that constitute this small, decaying watering-place which may, indeed, be called a 'backwater of life' without disrespect to its natives who possess, to this day, a salty individuality of their own ... The one place of worship, with its neglected graveyard, is of no architectural interest. (p. 19)

The words are wittily chosen: 'natives' as opposed to 'native inhabitants' and 'souls' as the unthinking cliché for merely counted heads. In such language, mention of the village's 'neglected graveyard', tucked in as it is with the point about the chapel's nondescript architecture, expresses merely antiquarian regret. One thing *Under Milk Wood* itself does not neglect is its graveyard.

Before turning to 'Return Journey' (1947), which is the next in the chronology of radio features that anticipate *Under Milk Wood*, we should not forget smaller scripts such as 'How to Begin a Story', 'Holiday Memory' and 'The Crumbs of One Man's Year' (all late 1946). They, too, are part of the picture, not least in revealing Thomas's knowledge of certain kinds of potential material. 'How to Begin a Story', for example, recognises 'the kind of story set in a small, lunatic area of Wessex, full of saintly or reprehensible vicars, wanton maidens, biblical sextons, and old men called Parsnip or Dottle':

> Mr Beetroot, that cracked though cosmic symbol of something or other, will, in the nutty village, with dialect, oafs, and potted sermons, conduct his investigation into unreal rural life. Everyone, in this sophisticatedly contrived bucolic morality, has his or her obsession: Minnie Worzel wants only the vicar; the vicar, the Reverend Nut, wants only the ghost of William Cowper to come into his brown study and read him 'The Task';

the Sexton wants worms; worms want the vicar. Lambkins, on those impossible hills, frolic, gambol, and are sheepish under the all-seeing eye of Uncle Teapot, the Celestial Tinker. Cruel farmers persecute old cow-herds called Crumpet, who talk, all day long, to cows; cows, tired of vaccine-talk in which they can have no part, gore, in a female manner, the aged relatives of cruel farmers; it is all very cosy in Upper Story. (*Broadcasts*, 125)

It is obviously a parody of T. F. Powys's fiction, with the talk of 'a small, lunatic area' and of 'the nutty village' carrying also a trace of the still latent 'Town That Was Mad' idea. It is material that *Under Milk Wood* recognises and transcends. In particular, the idea of everyone having 'his or her obsession' helped sharpen the one-character-one-theme simplicity of the play for voices.

But what the play capitalised on more than anything was an idea that in the broadcast 'Holiday Memory' was only a quick thought – 'if you could have listened at some of the open doors of some of the houses in the street you might have heard ...' (*Broadcasts*, 139). *Under Milk Wood* is ultimately about private worlds. And this inno-cent voyeurism was in turn what the broadcasts had inherited from techniques already exercised elsewhere in the prose and poetry. The formula of the onlooker or eavesdropper occurs in places where we don't even think of it as a formula. In 'Poem in October' (1944), for example:

> Myself to set foot
> That second
> In the still sleeping town...

Or in *Portrait of the Artist as a Young Dog* (1940):

I was a lonely night walker and a steady stander-at-corners. I liked to walk through the wet town after midnight, when the streets were deserted and the window lights out, alone under the moon, gigantically sad in damp streets by ghostly Ebenezer Chapel.

This self-conscious observer went back to Thomas's earliest mature prose. In 'The Orchards' (1936) the fact that the viewing artist is viewed is the main interest of the story: 'poor Marlais's morning, turning to evening, spins before you'. This interest in vantage-points was of course made more sophisticated by techniques Thomas later learned in writing for film. Camera-directions such as 'From our distance', 'Closer now', 'Closer still' and 'Coming closer to him' in the filmscript *The Doctor and the Devils* (1944) are precursors of *Under Milk Wood*'s 'Come closer now' and 'From where you are'. It now seems as if the darker material of the early stories could be at any moment transformed by the kindlier eye of the later artist – the following picture from 'The Horse's Ha' (1936),[16] for example:

> Butcher and baker fell asleep that night, their women sleeping at their sides ... Over the shops, the cold eggs that had life, the box where the rats worked all night on the high meat, the shopkeepers gave no thought of death.

On the road to Milk Wood, a stage in the transformation of such material was the comedy of the unfinished novel, *Adventures in the Skin Trade* (1941). This, for example, is surely already close to the spirit of *Under Milk Wood*:

> Mrs Probert next door, disguised as a she-goat in a night gown, butting the air with her Kirby grips; her dapper, commercial son, with a watch-chain tattooed across his rising belly; the tubercular lodger, with his neat umbrella up and his basin in his hand.

But, whether comic or not, where the omniscient *spectator ab extra* (seeing everything) merged most completely with the omniscient *auditor ab extra* (hearing everything) was in the particular medium of radio – where hearing *is* seeing.

Thomas would have read Edward Sackville-West's review of 'Holiday Memory' in the *New Statesman* (2 November 1946) which wondered 'why this remarkable poet has never attempted a poetic drama for broadcasting: he would seem to have all the qualities needed'. Thomas's first real move in that direction was 'Return Journey' (1947), his finest radio feature apart from *Under Milk Wood*. For one thing, 'Return Journey' opted for the extended use of a narrator, a feature of Thomas's play for radio that Raymond Williams, punning unconsciously, called 'a sound instinct'.[17] The dramatic advantage of a narrator was as a means of managing the interaction of a large range of characters on the stage of the listener's mind. But at the same time 'Return Journey' highlighted an important choice facing the author in the use of such an all-witnessing narrator. To what degree should the narrator become a character in his own right? The choice made in 'Return Journey' is clear. Its first-person Narrator is to all intents and purposes Thomas himself, searching for his Swansea childhood, buried under time and the rubble of the Blitz. The role of the narrator in *Under Milk Wood* is very different. The point can be made by way of the problem Andrew Sinclair found in producing his large-screen film version of the play in 1971, the problem of needing to ask –

> Who are the two voices? Why do they ride into town? Who are they looking for? Why do they leave town? What is their power of conjuring up dreams and the dead? This was never explained by Thomas, and it doesn't really matter when you're dealing with a form of incantation by voice, which it is as a radio play. But the moment you translate it into visual terms you are faced with a terrible choice. Now Dylan was writing in the forties style, and I think he was seduced by all those marvellous documentaries by Grierson and Jennings, when you had some terrific voice-over, and then you had a lot of beautiful picture postcards or views. But it's much later now – thirty years on – and it's no good doing a bloody travelogue of Wales, with pretty pictures and lovely voices over.[18]

This is to reap, with a vengeance, the dangers of too literally vis-ualising the play. Any externalisation beyond the magic-lantern of the mind or the barest stage-reading pushes us into giving the two Voices distinct characters, something they just do not have or need in the actual text. To solve his problem, Sinclair merged the play with two earlier works, the broadcast 'Return Journey' and the *Portrait* short story 'Just like Little Dogs', making the narrators two dead men returning to the town where they had loved the same girl. From as early as 'Brember' (1931), the tale of a man reclaiming his family history, the idea of a 'return journey' expressed something deep in Thomas's psychology. It is there in 'Quite Early One Morning', the work that otherwise most obviously resembles *Under Milk Wood*:

> Who lived in these cottages? I was a stranger to the sea town, fresh or stale from the city where I worked for my bread and butter wishing it were laver-bread and country salty butter yolk-yellow. (*Broadcasts*, 12)

The narrator of 'Quite Early One Morning' is clearly Dylan Thomas himself, tired of London ('the city of the restless dead') and beginning to recognise New Quay as one of those characterful islands his soul always needed to return to.

But the delightful thing about *Under Milk Wood*'s narration is exactly how motiveless it is and can afford to be. We don't for a moment wonder *why* we are being shown these things. We don't need a background to the foreground. The play depersonalises what had previously come through as the author's personal yearning to recall and reclaim. And yet the narration of *Under Milk Wood* isn't mere watching, mere listening, like the narrative of, say, 'The Londoner'. The play's narration is 'dramatic' in a specific sense: it exuberantly lives its way into the lives of others; it takes delight in what George Eliot called 'a superadded life in the life of others'; and takes, in Keats's phrase about the poetical character, 'as much delight in conceiving an Iago as an Imogen' – having itself 'no identity'. This offers an interesting comparison with an American work that Thomas greatly admired, Edgar Lee Masters's *Spoon River Anthology* (1915). This sequence of free-verse poems, each an epitaph spoken from the grave by former inhabitants of a small Mid-West town, reveals the complex interpenetration of public and private lives within a community. In late 1950, Thomas himself chose the book as the subject for a radio feature. Though the feature was not actually written until 1952, the choice of Masters's book in 1950 was significant because Thomas was at that time deciding on a plotless form for his own small-town portrait. There is not even a narrator in *Spoon River Anthology* and its author's motivating theme – what Thomas calls Masters's 'detestation of the bitter and crippling puritanism in which he struggled and simmered up' (*Broadcasts*, 257) – is allowed to emerge at a tangent from the monologues themselves. Though the theme of psychological repression is common to both works, Thomas's vision is of course tonally completely different. Affectionate rather than disaffected, it is closer to that of Sherwood Anderson's *Winesburg, Ohio* (1919), which Thomas quotes as a counter-balance to Masters's *Spoon River*, Anderson's work being 'more detailed and more gentle, in spite of its terrors' (*Broadcasts*, 257). But Thomas's vision in *Under Milk Wood* remains a vision, not a statement. As in *Spoon River Anthology*, the author's presence is communicated, not through narration, but through the emotive resonance of the work as a whole.

4

That is why we should remember the shadow of war in which Milk Wood grew. Thomas's delight at finally resettling in Laugharne in spring 1949 was in a classic literary-pastoral lineage, sad and escapist at one and the same time. Small Welsh places by the sea always tempered his fears without removing them; his laughter there was never thoughtless. Along with providing again character and atmosphere, post-war Laugharne prefigured the play's central paradox, that a place of doubtful repute can still be a 'place of love'. At heart, this search for innocence was in reaction to the Second World War, a fact that mainstreams the play with most of Thomas's poetry after 1939. Poems about innocent deaths in the London air-raids – in which the Luftwaffe claimed over 40,000 civilian lives, and in which Thomas was a fire-watcher – are among the poet's strongest utterances, made personally more painful by the bombing devastation of Swansea, a tragedy Thomas saw as the destruction of his very childhood. The deep sense of moral outrage in the war poems had often been linked to the death of children or the newly born:

> A child of a few hours
> With its kneading mouth
> Charred on the black breast of the grave
> The mother dug, and its arms full of fires.
>
> ('Ceremony after a Fire Raid')

But the war poems had also had about them a Churchillian resilience, a refusal to mourn. Ordinary people's conviction that prolonged conventional bombing would be unendurable – a fear common from as far back as H. G. Wells's *The War in the Air* (1908) but vividly driven home by propaganda in the 1930s – was in the upshot dispelled by Britain's brave, resilient survival in the Blitz. But the actual writing of *Under Milk Wood* was in a later phase of horror, in which the very perception of atrocity changed. A much deeper human insult was carried in news of the Nazi concentration camps, and the dropping of the atomic bomb on Hiroshima and Nagasaki in 1945 inaugurated a new dimension of horror. The Second World War was ended only by threatening an even more obscene Third, which not only renewed the concept of unlimitable deaths but made *cosmic* destruction feasible. After such knowledge, what forgiveness?

The legend of the irresponsible 'bohemian' surrounding Thomas has obscured the sense of moral shock at the heart of his later work. Virtually everything he wrote after the war expresses, directly or indirectly, a search for innocence. In 1945, in poems such as 'Fern Hill' and 'Poem in October' or the broadcast 'Memories of Christmas', he went back down the track of his own life to reclaim the basic optimism of childhood through the powers of art. This traditional remembrance of things past has often been criticised as regressive. But a concern for childhood is no less adult for being classic; in George Eliot's words, 'We could never have loved the earth so well if we had had no childhood in it.' But now the childhood of the very earth itself might be at hazard. Thomas's unfinished scheme for the large composite poem 'In Country Heaven' had as its premise that 'The Earth has killed itself. It is black, petrified, wizened, poisoned, burst; insanity has blown it rotten; and no creatures at all, joyful, despairing, cruel, kind, dumb, afire, loving, dull, no creatures at all shortly and brutishly hunt their days down like enemies on that corrupted face ... And the poem becomes, at last, an affirmation of the beautiful and terrible worth of the Earth' (*Broadcasts*, 225). The plot involved people having to re-imagine the simple joys of the earth from the other side of holocaust. It was the same loss-of-Eden theme that Philip Burton recognised when Thomas outlined to him the opera libretto he planned, on Aldous Huxley's recommendation, to write for Stravinsky.[19] To Stravinsky himself, Thomas outlined a plot in which humanity was faced with rediscovering not only love but language itself.[20] The collaboration with Stravinsky was to have started on the last fatal American visit of autumn 1953, a visit that also left the final part of *Under Milk Wood* incompletely realised.

The need to hang on to a concept of basic innocence in a hell-bent world is the background against which the warm humanity of the play has its profile. Thomas was already living in Laugharne when the Second World War – 'this war, trembling even on the edge of Laugharne' (*Collected Letters*, 401) – broke out. The congruence of place and time was crucial. 'When I Woke', a poem written in Laugharne on the very eve of war, had asked only for freedom to live and create:

> I heard, this morning, waking,
> Crossly out of the town noises
> A voice in the erected air,
> No prophet-progeny of mine,
> Cry my sea town was breaking.

It is through its very vulnerability that Laugharne, 'my sea town', became Llareggub, 'this place of love'. It is a place we know only in burgeoning springtime, which makes the play's prototype, 'Quite Early One Morning', in its cold winter setting, ultimately so dissimilar and, on its own, an inadequate forecast of the play's full resonance.

But the warm defence of human foibles in the face of greater evils is also what triggers in some quarters critical resistance to the play's appeal and quality, a resistance that makes it necessary to be clear about its exact genre. That the play's qualities as 'drama' are of a limited kind is something we should expect from its development out of the relaxed mode of the radio feature. But it is important to relax also any expectations regarding the work as 'sociology'. Even allowing for the importance of Laugharne as a model, Llareggub is not meant to be a community we could identify as an actual place, whose ethos we could imagine living by or worrying about. For that kind of equivalence, we look to different genres, the auto-biographical novel for example. But it is worth noting that the greatest Welsh-language novel of the century – Caradog Prichard's auto-biographical *Un Nos Ola Leuad* (*One Moonlit Night*, 1961), a painful picture of an actual north Wales slate-quarrying community losing its grip on outside reality – was first intended as a radio play in the manner of *Under Milk Wood*. It is uncannily as if Caradog Prichard had picked up the scent of the 'Town That Was Mad' idea even in the finished play. Beyond the 'play for voices' as a form, perhaps even the material has an authenticity that is adaptable in parts.

A vein of sociological appraisal – a reaction against hypocritical puritan 'respectability', for example – was always part of Thomas's prose, even at its most fantastical. But *Under Milk Wood* aims more at suggesting universal human nature than at delivering local lessons. Indeed, it is through that universalising of Welshness that it has run foul of modern Wales. Like all alert societies, Wales rightly resents the sabotage of its real self in the short-cuts of caricature, and though an implicit truce regarding *Under Milk Wood* was signed even across the language-barrier in the form of James Jones's excellent translation of the work into Welsh as *Dan y Wenallt* (1968), objections to the play's 'stage-Welshness' will always be understandable. Even Thomas would not have found the satire possible in quite this form in the more confident Wales that emerged in the 1960s. Similar issues were once raised by John Millington Synge's *The Playboy of the Western World* (1907), attacked not only for 'the brutishness and cowardice of its men and the coarseness of its women' but also because regional caricature lays national character open to ridicule. The same objec-tions lie behind the counter-attacks on Caradoc Evans, defending Cardiganshire against the libel of his fiction.[21] All such criticism is at base the one G. H. Lewes once made of Dickens – that his gallery of grotesques failed to evoke the complexity of an actual society.

But caricature is a time-honoured art, and Thomas would never have felt really defensive about it. In 'Living in Wales', a 1949 broadcast that uses many details that ultimately figured in *Under Milk Wood*, he pretends to mistrust his caricatures of the English even as he writes them:

Let me be fair, however much I dislike it. The men and women, and the others, in that [railway] carriage were not England. I do not point to one group of people, however repellent, and say, 'That, to me, is England. Help, let me out!' I distrust the man who says, 'Now *that* is England', and shows me a tailwag of rich tweedy women babytalking to their poodles. That is no more England than a village cricket match is. (*Broadcasts*, 203)

But the choice of a cricket match barbs the disclaimer. Certain things *are* quintessentially Welsh or English or Mid-West. And Thomas knew well enough that to call something 'mere caricature' is our instinctive response to anything that hits off our private weaknesses. Of Edgar Lee Masters's *Spoon River Anthology* he said that 'Many people read it in order to deny that it was true; many, discovering that in essence it was, denied it even more loudly. One of the chief reactions to these angry, sardonic, moving poems seemed to be: "*Some* of the inhabitants of small towns in Illinois may indeed be narrow-minded and corrupt, fanatically joyless, respectable to the point of insanity, malevolent and malcontent, but not in the Illinois towns in which *we* live"' (*Broadcasts*, 256). But the Reverend Eli Jenkins or Mrs Ogmore-Pritchard, or even the hypocritical Jack Black the cobbler, would never prompt the degree of regional-cum-national defensiveness that met Caradoc Evans's assaults on Welsh Non-conformity in the stories of *My People* (1915) and *Capel Sion* (1916). Even that disfiguring vision sprang from Evans's tortured love for Wales, but Thomas's characters don't seem designed to put anyone down in the first place, inside or outside the play.

The same criticism in less defensive form argues that such characters, whether regional or not, are hopelessly superficial. But this, too, fails to acknowledge *Under Milk Wood*'s real genre. Kenneth Tynan's insight, in his review of the 1956 Edinburgh Festival production, that the play is a 'true comedy of humours', involving only 'characters with one-track minds',[22] got the genre right early and at a stroke. A 'comedy of humours' blocks expectations of complex realism from the very start. It recognises instead something essentially formal, in which all is simplified foreground. But we have to remember that a simplified foreground can still carry a complex ground-tone. Sustained by narrator and character alike, the ground-tone in *Under Milk Wood* celebrates the simplest noises as if they were the Music of the Spheres –

There's the clip clop of horses on the sunhoneyed cobbles of the humming streets, hammering of horseshoes, gobble quack and cackle, tomtit twitter from the bird-ounced boughs, braying on Donkey Down. (p. 34)

Outside, the sun springs down on the rough and tumbling town. It runs through the hedges of Goosegog Lane, cuffing the birds to sing. Spring whips green down Cockle Row, and the shells ring out. Llareggub this snip of a morning is wildfruit and warm, the streets, fields, sands and waters springing in the young sun. (p. 36)

This harmony of the created and the man-made world merges in turn with the still sad music of humanity underlying it all. Any work that modulates so consistently between day and night, awake and asleep, youth and age, living and dead is bound to be, however comic, a *memento mori*. The play is a great celebration of 'creatures born to die' (p. 57), with the polarities of light and shadow balanced at every turn. The conflation of images of death with those of life has a particular frisson. An image obviously influenced by Stanley Spencer's resurrection paintings[23] has 'the dead come out in their Sunday best' (p. 61). The dead Rosie Probert who speaks to Captain Cat 'from the bedroom of her dust' (p. 51) spoke at one stage 'from the short-time bedroom of her dust', conflating her grave with cheap one-night hotels. The duality is maintained even in the lower-keyed sections, by a wonderfully inclusive use of language:

Dusk is drowned for ever until tomorrow. It is all at once night now. The windy town is a hill of windows, and from the larrupped waves, the lights of the lamps in the windows call back the day and the dead that have run away to sea. All over the calling dark, babies and old men are bribed and lullabied to sleep. (p. 59)

'Drowned', 'forever' and 'tomorrow' in the same brief sentence, and 'All at once', 'night' and 'now' in an even briefer one. Then the energy of 'windy', 'larrupped' and 'lights' refusing to let the day go gentle into night. And the polarity of it all epitomised in 'babies and old men', but given a lift by the witty inversion of having the babies 'bribed' and the old men 'lullabied'. It is brisk but capacious writing. And how poignant that metaphor for death as a running away to sea. It reminds us of our sea-town location, but also that it was youngsters who ran away to sea, and all too often died. Suddenly 'the dead that have run away to sea' ceases to be just a metaphor. At the same time, the lights calling back the dead remind us of the religious belief, now lost sight of in festivals such as Hallowe'en, that at certain times the souls of the dead return to their homes. It is in these rich resonances that we properly look for complexity. Otherwise, the only defence

Under Milk Wood needs is T. S. Eliot's defence of Ben Jonson's comedy:

> It is what it is; it does not pretend to be another thing. But it is so very conscious and deliberate that we must look with eyes alert to the whole before we apprehend the significance of any part. We cannot call a man's work superficial when it is the creation of a world; a man cannot be accused of dealing superficially with the world which he himself has created; the superficies *is* the world. Jonson's characters conform to the logic of the emotions of their world. They are not fancy, because they have a logic of their own; and this logic illuminates the actual world, because it gives us a new point of view from which to inspect it.[24]

The moment the first stage-reading proved *Under Milk Wood* a popular success, Thomas started talking of writing another 'play for voices'. But this would be a 'proper-er play' (*Collected Letters*, 893). An ordinary boy and girl from neighbouring streets in a Welsh industrial town would meet only at the end of their lives, too late for love.[25] It seems a desire to push the safety of *Under Milk Wood* out into a realer, a 'proper-er' world. In the meantime Llareggub was, quite properly, its own world.

Notes in Thomas's worksheets, emphasising how innocuous is each character's effect on another, show how psychologically uncloying the play was meant to be from the start. The play's lovers can live neither with nor without each other, which both contradicts and confirms Marvell's claim in 'The Garden' that 'Two Paradises 'twere in one/To live in Paradise alone'. The love between Mog Edwards and Myfanwy Price, for example, depends on their never meeting, and the relationship between Mr and Mrs Cherry Owen relies on his being two husbands, one for the daytime, another for the night. Such simplifying processes make *Under Milk Wood* a version of pastoral, Llareggub a comic paradise. The worksheets at Texas spell out the benign, closed-circuit effect of these relationships. The note on Mr and Mrs Pugh, for example: 'Both are satisfied. If he had married a woman who did not nag, he would have little justification to plot against her. And she, who knows well his thoughts, would be miserable too, having nothing to do.' Or the note on Willy Nilly the postman: 'Nobody minds him opening the letters and acting as [a] kind of town-crier. How else could they know the news?' Such blithe acceptance confirms a general 'blessing on the town' (p. 57) and in that sense Thomas really does speak through the Reverend Eli Jenkins. Similar worksheet blessings occur for Organ Morgan, Dai Bread and his two wives, Mrs Ogmore-Pritchard, Jack Black, Mr Waldo, Nogood Boyo, and Butcher Beynon and his wife. One of them got into the final text as a specific apologia – the one stressing that Organ Morgan's mad night-time organ-playing is at least entertainment for 'anyone who will listen': lovers, revellers, the silent dead, tramps, and even sheep (p. 61). The mitigating pen-portraits in the worksheets, shamelessly cutting the tricky human corners of poisonous thoughts and opened letters, were Thomas's reminders to himself to keep the characters on course for forgiveness.

He had originally planned to quote each one of these simplifying verdicts as if it were a quotation from the Reverend Eli Jenkins's own 'White Book of Llareggub'. In a note marked 'VERY important', he planned to 'Refer, towards the end, to the White Book of Llareggub (mentioning the Black Book of Llanstephan)' for references about the natural moral innocence of all the above inhabitants. The 'warm White Book of Llareggub' (with 'warm White' suggesting interior decorating rather than cold history) is the Reverend Eli Jenkins's 'Lifework' (pp. 54, 62). Though meant to be a book about 'the Population, Main Industry, Shipping, History, Topography, Flora and Fauna of the town he worships in', a book in which he 'tells only the truth', it is in fact the opposite, a work that repersonalises the depersonalised facts of Information Books and Guidebooks. In the upshot, the only characters actually cited as if from the pages of Eli Jenkins's book are Mog Edwards and Myfanwy Price, and the one literal innocent, the village idiot Bessie Bighead:

> Look up Bessie Bighead in the White Book of Llareggub and you will find the few haggard rags and the one poor glittering thread of her history laid out in pages there with as much love and care as the lock of hair of a first lost love. (p. 55)

Had Thomas carried out his plan of defending the others, too, by this mock appeal to Eli Jenkins's chronicle, the effect of summing-up would have helped rationalise the play's rather precipitate close. But it would also have made that close more apologetic than it needs to be. The diffused, contagious innocence of it all is by that stage already established. We are riding the ball by then.

But the play might well have turned out darker. Many unused ideas in the Texas manuscripts show Thomas contemplating certain shades and shadows not now associated with the work:

> Bring in Tom [later Sinbad] the Sailor's hopeless love for Gossamer

Beynon. Gossamer's erotic dreams. The tragedy behind Lord Cut Glass's life. The sadness of No-good Boyo. The terrible jealously of Mrs Cherry. Mrs Ogmor-Pritchard's terrible death-waiting loneliness. The poverty of the town, the idiocy, the incest. Look at the graveyard: remember the early mortality and fatalities. This all to show Llareggub no Utopia.

Immediately after this, Thomas wrote 'Huge donkeybray, close to mike' – so different from the present sound-effects of cockcrows, bell-notes and organ-music. Sinbad Sailors' hopeless love and Gossamer Beynon's erotic dreams did get in, to good comic effect, as in the latter's dream of 'a small rough ready man with a bushy tail winking in a paper carrier' (p. 14). But 'the tragedy behind Lord Cut Glass's life' or 'Mrs Ogmore-Pritchard's terrible death-waiting loneliness' is hardly how those characters were developed. In connection with what Thomas calls 'the poverty of the town, the idiocy, the incest', it is interesting to see him asking on another worksheet 'What have I missed out?' and then listing 'Incest/Greed/Hate/Envy/Spite/Malice', followed again by the reminder in capital letters to 'STRESS THE FEAR OF SOME OF THE TOWN AFTER DARK'. In the same tone, an injunction to 'look at the graveyard' and 'remember the early mortality and fatalities' is a vestige of Edgar Lee Masters's *Spoon River Anthology*, all spoken from such a graveyard, but in an infinitely more acidic elegy than *Under Milk Wood* turned out to be. Thomas's kind of elegy – warm even when heartbreaking, closer to Thomas Hardy than to Edgar Lee Masters – is established by the very first characters to speak, the drowned sailors who nuzzle up to the sleeping Captain Cat. It is one of the very finest sections of the play, the one T. S. Eliot particularly admired,[26] resonating memorably on deceptively simple details as the drowned sailors wonder 'How's it above?':

> THIRD DROWNED
> How's the tenors in Dowlais?

> FOURTH DROWNED
> Who milks the cows in Maesgwyn?

> FIFTH DROWNED
> When she smiles, is there dimples?

> FIRST DROWNED
> What's the smell of parsley? (p. 4)

The old adage comes to mind – if a work is to end badly, it should end badly from the start. When darker 'suggestions' (Thomas's term in the worksheets) were not in harmony with the affirmative tenor quickly established by the play, they were finally kept at bay – for example, the suggestion that he 'Bring in, whenever [Evans] the Death is introduced, his mother' and give him a 'mother-love' song in a section planned for the evening in the pub. An obsessive link between death and the mother, though potent in the imagery of the poems, is not something the final play leaves with us. Evans the Death's dream of seeing, as a child, his mother 'making Welshcakes in the snow' (p. 8) is lyrical and visionary, not trapped and ruinous. Also unused was the following poignant but odd suggestion involving Eli Jenkins:

God is love, the Reverend Eli Jenkins tells a parishioner dying. Hod is Love? the old woman whispers. Yea, Hod is Love, he says with reverence. And she flies from a hovel to a mansion, quick as a simple flash.

Eli Jenkins's refusal to be worried at such a time by mere semantics is true to his character, and to the general forgiving tenor of the play, whose concern is with what a Thomas poem calls 'unjudging love'. And yet Eli Jenkins's 'Yea, Hod is Love' would still have jarred the tone of the *Under Milk Wood* we now know. It suggests an existentialist, inconsequential world very different from the simple inconsequence of having 'God is Love' hang above the bigamous bed of Dai Bread and his two wives (p. 40). Thomas's note to himself that these darker suggestions are 'all to show Llareggub no Utopia' is on worksheets where he also considered a final night sequence ('Midnight/ the dead come out . . .') in which 'Llareggub is buggerall now'. But the optimistic logic of the work was too powerful. Llareggub *is* a Utopia, an Eden, an Arcadia – a sexual and satiric one, yes, but with a moral force that does not depend on having its air of fun and unreality darkly sabotaged.

The copious worksheets show the rich inventiveness out of which the play was finally distilled. Only a richly talented writer can afford to leave unused a phrase like the one describing Mrs Organ Morgan snoring 'soft and silent as a needle drawn through water': in fact, only a writer with the talent to describe, instead, Mr Organ Morgan snoring 'no louder than a spider' (p. 17). Also important were plans to extend the final evening section. Sending his literary agent a copy of the version used in the May 1953 performance in New York, Thomas said that 'it will be seen that *dusk* arrives too sharply and suddenly and that the whole of the day *up to* the dusk much overbalances, in emphasis and bulk, the day *after* dusk' (*Collected Letters*, 904). The main plan for extending the evening of the play was to expand the section in the Sailors Arms by writing songs for Nogood Boyo, Mary Ann the Sailors, Evans the Death and Lily Smalls.[27] Thomas's death means that the late pub scene resounds only with Mr Waldo's sturdy ballad 'In Pembroke City when I was young', an excellent example of the play's sharp and varied use of song:

> Did you ever hear of a growing boy
> To live so cruel cheap
> On grub that has no flesh and bones
> And liquor that makes you weep? (p. 60)

But we should not assume that the additional songs would definitely have been used, or that they were structurally necessary. The vivid gusto of the parts, the burst of human colour, might even have been dulled and diluted by a concern for abstract proportions. The very freshness of the piece may depend on its having turned out, in that respect, 'no better than it should be' (p. 24). Thomas realised that extending the close was certainly not something demanded by the play in performance: it was already 'about as much as, in my opinion, an audience could be expected to take' (*Collected Letters*, 904). From summer 1953 onwards, plans to add to the close were stimulated more than anything by thoughts about the play as a text to be read: 'I am now *adding* quite a lot to this, and changing quite a bit which is more effective on the stage, I think, than it would be on the printed page ... It can be made to *look* quite a nice book, I think'. For stage-reading or radio, adjusting the balance between morning, afternoon and evening would have meant sacrificing some of the morning and afternoon material. Simply extending the final third was only feasible if one thought of the play as a text to be read.

5

It is of course as readers that we most frequently experience the play. But our reading is richer if it also *hears* the work, as a 'play for voices'. It has by now been projected through many different media – from early intimations in the prose and poetry and the radio features through to the radio play itself; from two classic early recordings and endless stage-readings through to a big-screen film in 1971 and an EMI celebrity recording in 1988. The most recent of its extended forms was perhaps the most inevitable – the S4C animated-film version, which matches the 'cartoon' simplicity on which the play itself so thrives. But it is its radio-ness we should keep in mind or, better still, its *wireless*-ness. Like 'skyscraper', the word 'wireless' takes us back to the creative period itself. Just as with buildings *scraping the sky*, the idea of mankind speaking on the air *without wires* still retained some wonder. In one of his broadcasts, Thomas could wittily still affect surprise at 'this, to me, unbelievable lack of wires' (*Broadcasts*, 225) that was at that very moment carrying his words. The myriad sophistications described in the 'Technical Details' of the EMI celebrity recording of 1988[28] seem positively futuristic compared with the simplicity of the BBC's 'Rehearsals' memo for the original broadcast of 1954. On the BBC file-copy of the latter, a technician has written 'For ethereal echo get Control Room to insert a basefilter on output of microphone to feed to echo chamber (as in Manchester Children's Hour)'. Though technically relatively straight-forward, the original 1954 broadcast of *Under Milk Wood* still seemed most wonderful. It was a different world.

The crucial part of that difference was the potent radio culture to which the play first belonged. What the *TLS* reviewer (5 March 1954) of the first printed edition appreciated was the fact that Thomas had 'developed a brisk comic style closely resembling that of Itma':

> *A mogul catches Lily Smalls in the wash-house.*

> LILY SMALLS
> Ooh, you old mogul!

> *Mrs Rose-Cottage's eldest, Mae, peels off her pink-and-white skin in a furnace in a tower in a cave in a waterfall in a wood and waits there raw as an onion for Mister Right to leap up the burning tall hollow splashes of leaves like a brilliantined trout.*

> MAE ROSE-COTTAGE
> [Very close and softly, drawing out the words.]
> Call me Dolores
> Like they do in the stories. (p. 16)

The reviewer's reference to 'Itma' (It's that Man Again) helps us reconstruct the wider cultural moment. Tommy Handley's immensely popular comic series, which ran for 310 programmes from 1939 to 1949, epitomised the part which radio entertainment of the 1940s and early 1950s played in assuaging the cold realities of war and its aftermath. In many ways the great decade of radio was the 1930s. By the time radio had become *the* medium it was overtaken by the Second World War, which then gave it an applied role to play. The media heroes of the 1940s were the war-correspondents, who had to find equally swift routes to the listener's attention. In this sense Thomas knew what he was doing when he worked into his broadcasts self-referential points regarding the role of wireless itself. In 'The Londoner' in 1946, for example, Ted Jackson says that during the war he used to make wireless sets only in order to dismantle them, never listening for 'more than a couple of minutes'. But during the three years that Ted Jackson was a prisoner of war, says his wife Lily, 'I used to hear his voice in the silly old dance tunes they played on the wireless, but the words weren't silly any more' (*Broadcasts*, 85–6). The post-war period in which the wireless slowly came back into its own (though still reflecting a world in crisis) was a phase to which Thomas himself richly contributed. The slow growth of *Under Milk Wood*, however, meant that, by the time its example could have encouraged similar works, not only was Thomas dead, but wireless itself as a mass resource was giving way to television. But in that cultural moment just before television's final ascendance, the wireless still had a visionary if visionless confidence in its outreach.

It is a confidence that *Under Milk Wood* now recreates in us. Not just by telling us, in the age of satellites and e-mail, 'Only your eyes are unclosed, to see' and 'you alone can hear' (p. 3), and not just by making blind Captain Cat our sightless, alertly listening, proxy within the play. A radio drama is by its very nature synchronic, in the strict sense of everything coinciding in time but not in place. And therefore, just as within the work dreams are co-inhabited by villagers otherwise separated by streets, mistrust, class, respectability and even death, so we too as listeners cross a physical space closed only by voices. All the more solidly to fill that space, Thomas employs simple devices to give the material mass as well as speed. If certain details seem as if we have met them before, it's because we have. For example, when Mr Waldo dreams of gossiping neighbours accusing him of selling the pianola and the sewing machine (p. 10), we half remember the Fifth Drowned confessing to Captain Cat in his dream that 'it was me that pawned the ormolu clock' (p. 5). When the same neighbours accuse Mr Waldo as a boy of 'stealing currants' (p. 11), we half recall Evans the Death waking in a dream and stealing currants from his mother (p. 8). That very oddity of 'waking in a dream' returns when Mrs Ogmore-Pritchard, too, wakes in a dream (p. 12) or when (a deft variation) Mr Pugh, 'fast asleep, pretends to be sleeping' (p. 17).

These doublings and double-takes involve us in the dream psychology of that particular part of the play. But they also occur outside the dreams. The fact that Lily Smalls' breath 'clouds the shaving-glass' (p. 22) is somehow still there when Mrs Dai Bread Two's crystal ball also clouds over (p. 41). In this way, the 'play for voices' is closer to a lyric poem than to a play. Like a lyric, it plotlessly circles around an unstated centre, always husbanding its own best effects, always threatening to round back to where it started, then actually doing so. Thomas knew exactly what he was saying when he called it 'an entertainment out of the darkness' (*Collected Letters*, 813). In not completely finalising itself in a plot, or externalising itself on to page or stage or screen, the voices across the air create a kind of unattached, self-sustaining music. As you listen, all the play's resources are within you. In T. S. Eliot's words, 'you *are* the music while the music lasts'.[29]

The evanescence of a 'play for voices' means that it has to be linguistically all the more vivid. And the very paradox of a *vivid evanescence* is written into the play in self-referential touches throughout, as through a stick of seaside rock. The very first word – 'Silence' – threatens the world of sound by which a 'play for voices' lives. In a playful awareness of its own form, the play then continues to threaten itself with words notionally on their way back towards silence – 'muffled', 'lulled', 'dumbfound', 'hushed', 'dumb', 'gloved', 'furred'. In one section at one stage Thomas considered teasing our very dependence on words, by evoking their opposite in the wordlessness of dreams:

> Mrs Rose-Cottage's eldest, Mae, is dreaming of dreaming of tall, tower, white, furnace, cave, flower, ferret, waterfall, sigh, without any words at all.

But though radio is a good medium for the quick montage of dreams, Thomas must have recognised that those staccato words would have come through as mere words, not brisk pictures. He re-wrote the passage so that we are led through the discrete words into a delightfully indiscreet picture:

> Mrs Rose-Cottage's eldest, Mae, peels off her pink-and-white skin in a furnace in a tower in a cave in a waterfall in a wood and waits there raw as an onion for Mister Right to leap up the burning tall hollow splashes of leaves like a brilliantined trout. (p. 16)

In these ways the act of seeing is never taken for granted. The very fact that this radio play starts and ends with night makes the medium the message. Beyond the words, there is, literally, only a non-seeing. As a friend of Richard Hughes, Thomas knew that the very first play specifically produced for radio was Hughes's *A Comedy of Danger* (1924), set in the pitch black of a coal mine after an accident.[30] Everything in such works depends, in Captain Cat's wonderful phrase, on 'the noise of the hush' (p. 33), on what *Under Milk Wood* also calls a 'calling dark' (p. 59). Using a clever inversion of the ordinary question, *Can you hear me from there?*, the play repeatedly tells us that 'From where you are you can hear ...' – 'where you are', of course, being the only place where you *can* hear. When we are later momentarily threatened ('all too far away for him, or you, to hear', p. 29), we all the more alertly cling to our station. Our natural human curiosity wants that heard darkness to be a darkness visible. It is the instinct that makes John Wain's poem 'Blind Man Listening to Radio' and Philip Larkin's poem 'Broadcast' so true. In Larkin's poem a girl-friend is at a broadcast concert to which the poet is listening. He finds himself imagining, beyond the blind air-waves, her 'gloves unnoticed on the floor'. The applause at the end leaves him even

> desperate to pick out
> Your hands, tiny in all that air, applauding.

Our ability to reach through the heard word to the seen picture is what energises the play. On the very first page we are asked to imagine a wood 'limping invisible down' to the sea. In the cliché, what woods normally do is *run down* to the sea. The change in the cliché revivifies it, tempting us for the first time to *see* it. On the very last page, we are told that a breeze 'sighs the streets' close under Milk Wood. We might not feel prompted overmuch to imagine the sound of a sigh, but that the breeze comes from 'the creased water' is something we suddenly visualise, as clearly as the 'tear-splashed blush' of the bullied boy in the children's forfeiting game (p. 45). Beyond these small touches, the language is all the while considering and leading us into the multiple angles from which things are visible in the first place. Hence Lily Smalls's view of her own face in Mr Beynon's shaving-glass (p. 21) or the view the airborne morning seagulls have of Dai Bread hurrying to the bakery (p. 23), reversed as it is later in Willy Nilly's view 'in sudden Springshine' of 'herring gulls heckling down to the harbour' (p. 38). These varying perspectives are shared out and interchanged between narrator and character like angles between different cameras:

> MRS PUGH
> ... Has Mr Jenkins said his poetry?
>
> MR PUGH
> Yes, dear.
>
> MRS PUGH
> Then it's time to get up. Give me my glasses. No, not my *reading* glasses, I want to look *out*. I want to see

Lily Smalls the treasure down on her red knees washing the front step. (pp. 22–3)

Lily Smalls is only the first of a series of main characters whom Mrs Pugh then 'sees', like a camera, on our behalf. Radio is reminding us of film. Like Mrs Pugh, we too must be careful not to keep only our 'reading glasses' on. When we read on the first page that 'Young girls lie bedded soft or glide in their dreams, with rings and trousseaux, bridesmaided by glow-worms down the aisles of the organplaying wood', we should remember that Thomas was a keen film fan. Glow-worms as bridesmaids and trees like a cartoon version of organ-pipes – everything no doubt swaying and bulging musically – it is pure Walt Disney.

But these effects are only possible because the words on the page have already the heart of the matter in them. One of the things about *Under Milk Wood* is the sheer number of expressions which, though quietly at home when we read or hear them, have a memorability that makes them also return singly to the mind. On reflection, we can identify the kink in their logic that makes each one memorable. We can even grade the degree of their logical off-centredness. The description of night, for example, going through the graveyard 'with winds gloved and folded' (p. 4) is by simple analogy with the folded wings of the carved angels there. Slightly more puzzling might be Mog Edwards's boast that he will take Myfanwy Price away to his Emporium on the hill 'where the change hums on wires' (p. 7), an image that memorialises a feature of the posh shops of an era that was coming to an end with the play itself. But what of Eli Jenkins's sudden plea, 'Oh, angels be careful there with your knives and forks'? It is a one-liner whose connections to its immediate context seem positively surrealistic. Eli Jenkins is writing before a photograph of his late mother:

*His mother, propped against a pot in a palm, with her wedding-ring waist
and bust like a blackcloth diningtable, suffers in her stays.*

REV. ELI JENKINS
Oh, angels be careful there with your knives and forks,

*he prays. There is no known likeness of his father Esau, who, undog-
collared because of his little weakness, was scythed to the bone one harvest
by mistake when sleeping with his weakness in the corn.*   (pp. 54–5)

Is the sudden 'Oh, angels be careful there with your knives and forks'
prompted by the 'diningtable', by the mother's piercing corsets, or by
the memory of the father's unfortunate encounter with the scythe?
The line surely galvanises all three. The baseline for such brilliant
strokes is the vivid life invested in even the simplest phrases throughout the play: in Gossamer Beynon's not caring if Sinbad Sailors *is*
common 'so long as he's all cucumber and hooves' (p. 46), for
example, or Captain Cat's memory of 'Lazy early Rosie with the
flaxen thatch' (p. 51).

Thomas's only direction to the five nervous but resourceful American actors who joined him in the first stage-readings in New York in
May and October 1953 was 'Love the words, love the words'. He
would himself have relished a particular touch in John Malcolm
Brinnin's description of the play's première in May 1953 at the Poetry
Center in New York.[31] In an image appropriately tinged by the
play's marriage of hearing and seeing, Brinnin unconsciously merged
'breath', the source of words, with 'light', the means of sight:

The stage was dim until a soft breath of light showed Dylan's face: 'To
begin at the beginning'.

WALFORD DAVIES

References

1   Elizabeth Reitell was John Malcolm Brinnin's assistant at the Poetry
    Center of the Young Men's and Young Women's Hebrew Association
    in New York. Thomas's comment was quoted by her in a letter to
    Daniel Jones (20 July 1954) now in the possession of the Trustees of
    the Dylan Thomas Estate.

2   Dylan Thomas, *The Collected Letters*, ed. Paul Ferris, Dent 1985,
    p. 772. Hereafter cited as *Collected Letters* within the text.

3 Cynthia Davis, 'The Voices of "Under Milk Wood" ', *Criticism* 17 (1975) 74–89 does not make a convincing case for distinct qualities in the voices.

4 John Malcolm Brinnin, *Dylan Thomas in America*, Dent 1956, p. 103.

5 'Dylan Thomas's Play for Voices', *The Critical Quarterly* 1 (Spring 1959) p. 26.

6 Kent Thompson, *Dylan Thomas in Swansea* (unpublished Ph.D. thesis, University of Wales, Swansea, 1965) p. 299.

7 See Introduction by Douglas Cleverdon to J. Stevens Cox (ed.), *Under Milk Wood: Account of an Action to Recover the Original Manuscript*, The Toucan Press, Guernsey, C.I., 1969.

8 T. Gwynn Jones, 'Dialects' in *A History of Carmarthenshire*, ed. Sir J. E. Lloyd for the London Carmarthenshire Society, two vols. 1935, vol. 1, p. 20. The character of Laugharne, especially its own sense of uniqueness, is even more vividly evoked in Mary Curtis's *The Antiquities of Laugharne, Pendine, and their Neighbourhoods* (1880, expanded from a shorter volume of 1871), published in a facsimile reprint by Dyfed County Council's Cultural Services Department in 1991.

9 Contribution by Richard Hughes to *Portrait of Dylan Thomas*, a BBC Third Programme tribute on 9 November 1963.

10 Caitlin Thomas with George Tremlett, *Caitlin: Life with Dylan Thomas*, Secker and Warburg 1986, pp. 118–21.

11 BBC Written Archives Centre, Caversham.

12 Dylan Thomas, *The Notebook Poems 1930–1934*, ed. Ralph Maud, Dent 1989, p. 254.

13 Constantine FitzGibbon, *The Life of Dylan Thomas*, Dent 1965, p. 269.

14 Dylan Thomas, *The Broadcasts*, ed. Ralph Maud, Dent 1991, p. 11. Hereafter cited as *Broadcasts* within the text.

15 Douglas Cleverdon, *The Growth of Milk Wood*, Dent 1969, p. 19. Hereafter cited as *Cleverdon* within the text.

16 Dylan Thomas, *Early Prose Writings*, ed. Walford Davies, Dent 1971, p. 37; *Dylan Thomas: The Collected Stories*, ed. Walford Davies, Dent 1983, p. 63.

17 'Dylan Thomas's Play for Voices', p. 20.

18 John Hall, 'The Magic of Milk Wood' [based on an interview with Andrew Sinclair], *Guardian Weekly*, 29 May 1971, p. 20.

19 *The Legend and the Poet*, ed. E. W. Tedlock, Heineman (and Mercury Books) 1963, pp. 69–70.

20 'Stravinsky and Dylan Thomas', chapter 4 of Robert Craft, *Stravinsky: Glimpse of a Life*, Limetree 1992, p. 55.

21 The best responses, even by native inhabitants of the same area as Caradoc Evans, are by no means simple cases of taking umbrage. They explore, instead, the cultural richness and complexity of the actual community that fell prey to Evans's caricature. See, for example, David Jenkins, 'Community and Kin: Caradoc Evans "At Home"', *The Anglo-Welsh Review*, vol. 24, no. 53 (Winter 1974), pp. 43–57.

22 Kenneth Tynan, 'Welsh Wizardry', *The Observer*, 26 August 1956, p. 10.

23 The most obvious is *The Resurrection: Port Glasgow* (1950), now in the Tate Gallery, London.

24 T. S. Eliot, 'Ben Jonson' in *Selected Essays*, 1932, p. 156.

25 As told to John Malcolm Brinnin – *Dylan Thomas in America*, pp. 176–77; as told to Philip Burton – *Dylan Thomas: The Legend and the Poet*, ed. E. W. Tedlock, pp. 68–9.

26 Vernon Watkins, in conversation with Walford Davies.

27 The Texas worksheets also show that, elsewhere, poems were contemplated for Lord Cut-Glass and Gossamer Beynon.

28 'Technical Details' in the comprehensive (untitled) brochure accompanying the launch of the recording in 1988. In the same brochure, see Jon Jacobs's 'The Engineer's Soundings'.

29 T. S. Eliot, 'The Dry Salvages', *Four Quartets*.

30 Richard Hughes, 'The Birth of Radio Drama', *The Atlantic Monthly*, December 1957. Reprinted in *Fiction as Truth: Selected Literary Writings by Richard Hughes*, ed. Richard Poole, Poetry Wales Press, Bridgend, 1983, pp. 32–7.

31 *Dylan Thomas in America*, p. 174.

UNDER MILK WOOD

A PLAY FOR VOICES

SILENCE

st VOICE : (very softly)

To begin at the beginning:

It is spring, moonless night in the small town, starless and bible-black, the cobblestreets silent and the hunched, courters'-and-rabbits' wood limping invisible down to the sloeblack, slow, black, crowblack, fishingboat-bobbing sea. The houses are blind as moles (though moles see fine tonight in the snouting, velvet dingles) or blind as Captain Cat there in the muffled middle by the pump and the town clock, the shops in mourning, the Welfare Hall in widows' weeds. And all the people of the ~~town~~ lulled and dumbfound town are sleeping now.

Hush, the babies are sleeping, the farmers, the fishers, the tradesmen and pensioners, cobbler, schoolteacher, postman and publican, the undertaker and the fancy woman, drunkard, ~~dressmaker~~, preacher, policeman, the webfoot cocklewomen and the tidy wives. Young girls lie bedded soft or glide in their dreams, with rings and trousseaux, bridesmaided by glow-worms down the aisles of the organplaying wood. The boys are dreaming wicked or of the bucking ranches of the night and the jolly, rodgered sea. And the anthracite statues of the horses sleep in the fields, and the cows in the byres, and the dogs in the wetnosed yards; and the cats nap in the slant corners or lope sly, streaking and needling, on the one cloud of the roofs.

You can hear the dew falling, and the hushed town breathing.

Holograph opening of Under Milk Wood

[Silence]

FIRST VOICE [Very softly]

To begin at the beginning:

It is spring, moonless night in the small town, starless and bible-black, the cobblestreets silent and the hunched, courters'-and-rabbits' wood limping invisible down to the sloeblack, slow, black, crowblack, fishingboat-bobbing sea. The houses are blind as moles (though moles see fine tonight in the snouting, velvet dingles) or blind as Captain Cat there in the muffled middle by the pump and the town clock, the shops in mourning, the Welfare Hall in widows' weeds. And all the people of the lulled and dumbfound town are sleeping now.

Hush, the babies are sleeping, the farmers, the fishers, the tradesmen and pensioners, cobbler, schoolteacher, postman and publican, the undertaker and the fancy woman, drunkard, dressmaker, preacher, policeman, the webfoot cocklewomen and the tidy wives. Young girls lie bedded soft or glide in their dreams, with rings and trousseaux, bridesmaided by glow-worms down the aisles of the organplaying wood. The boys are dreaming wicked or of the bucking ranches of the night and the jolly, rodgered sea. And the anthracite statues of the horses sleep in the fields, and the cows in the byres, and the dogs in the wetnosed yards; and the cats nap in the slant corners or lope sly, streaking and needling, on the one cloud of the roofs.

You can hear the dew falling, and the hushed town breathing.

Only your eyes are unclosed, to see the black and folded town fast, and slow, asleep.

And you alone can hear the invisible starfall, the darkest-before-dawn minutely dewgrazed stir of the black, dab-filled sea where the Arethusa, the Curlew and the Skylark, Zanzibar, Rhiannon, the Rover, the Cormorant, and the Star of Wales tilt and ride.

Listen. It is night moving in the streets, the processional salt slow musical wind in Coronation Street and Cockle Row, it is the grass *growing on Llareggub Hill, dewfall, starfall, the sleep of birds in Milk Wood.*

Listen. It is night in the chill, squat chapel, hymning, in bonnet and brooch and bombazine black, butterfly choker and bootlace bow, coughing like nannygoats, sucking mintoes, fortywinking hallelujah; night in the four-ale, quiet as a domino; in Ocky Milkman's loft like a mouse with gloves; in Dai Bread's bakery flying like black flour. It is tonight in Donkey Street, trotting silent, with seaweed on its hooves, along the cockled cobbles, past curtained fernpot, text and trinket, harmonium, holy dresser, watercolours done by hand, china dog and rosy tin teacaddy. It is night neddying among the snuggeries of babies.

Look. It is night, dumbly, royally winding through the Coronation cherry trees; going through the graveyard of Bethesda with winds gloved and folded, and dew doffed; tumbling by the Sailors' Arms.

Time passes. Listen. Time passes.

Come closer now.

Only you can hear the houses sleeping in the streets in the slow deep salt and silent black, bandaged night. Only you can see, in the blinded bedrooms, the coms and petticoats over the chairs, the jugs and basins, the glasses of teeth, Thou Shalt Not on the wall, and the yellowing dickybird-watching pictures of the dead. Only you can hear and see, behind the eyes of the sleepers, the movements and countries and mazes and colours and dismays and rainbows and tunes and wishes and flight and fall and despairs and big seas of their dreams.

From where you are, you can hear their dreams.

Captain Cat, the retired blind seacaptain, asleep in his bunk in the seashelled, ship-in-bottled, shipshape best cabin of Schooner House dreams of
           never such seas as any that swamped the decks of his S.S. Kidwelly bellying over the bedclothes and jellyfish-slippery sucking him down salt deep into the Davy dark where the fish come biting out and nibble him down to his wishbone and the long drowned nuzzle up to him...

FIRST DROWNED
Remember me, Captain?

CAPTAIN CAT
You're Dancing Williams!

FIRST DROWNED
I lost my step in Nantucket.

SECOND DROWNED
Do you see me, Captain? the white bone talking?
I'm Tom-Fred the donkeyman ... We shared the
same girl once ... Her name was Mrs Probert...

WOMAN'S VOICE
Rosie Probert, thirty three Duck Lane. Come on up,
boys, I'm dead.

THIRD DROWNED
Hold me, Captain, I'm Jonah Jarvis, come to a bad
end, very enjoyable...

FOURTH DROWNED
Alfred Pomeroy Jones, sealawyer, born in Mumbles,
sung like a linnet, crowned you with a flagon, tattooed with mermaids, thirst like a dredger, died of
blisters...

FIRST DROWNED
This skull at your earhole is

FIFTH DROWNED
Curly Bevan. Tell my auntie it was me that pawned
the ormolu clock...

CAPTAIN CAT
Aye, aye, Curly.

SECOND DROWNED
Tell my missus no my never

THIRD DROWNED
I never done what she said I never...

FOURTH DROWNED
Yes, they did.

FIFTH DROWNED
And who brings cocoanuts and shawls and parrots
to *my* Gwen now?

FIRST DROWNED

How's it above?

SECOND DROWNED

Is there rum and lavabread?

THIRD DROWNED

Bosoms and robins?

FOURTH DROWNED

Concertinas?

FIFTH DROWNED

Ebenezer's bell?

FIRST DROWNED

Fighting and onions?

SECOND DROWNED

And sparrows and daisies?

THIRD DROWNED

Tiddlers in a jamjar?

FOURTH DROWNED

Buttermilk and whippets?

FIFTH DROWNED

Rock-a-bye baby?

FIRST DROWNED

Washing on the line?

SECOND DROWNED

And old girls in the snug?

THIRD DROWNED

How's the tenors in Dowlais?

FOURTH DROWNED

Who milks the cows in Maesgwyn?

FIFTH DROWNED

When she smiles, is there dimples?

FIRST DROWNED

What's the smell of parsley?

CAPTAIN CAT
Oh, my dead dears!

From where you are, you can hear, in Cockle Row in the spring,
moonless night, Miss Price, dressmaker and sweetshop-keeper, dream of
her lover, tall as the town clock tower, Samson-
syrup-gold-maned, whacking thighed and piping hot, thunderbolt-bass'd
and barnacle-breasted flailing up the cockles with his eyes like blowlamps
and scooping low over her lonely loving hotwaterbottled body...

MR EDWARDS
Myfanwy Price!

MISS PRICE
Mr Mog Edwards!

MR EDWARDS
I am a draper mad with love. I love you more than
all the flannelette and calico, candlewick, dimity,
crash and merino, tussore, cretonne, crepon, muslin,
poplin, ticking and twill in the whole Cloth Hall of
the world. I have come to take you away to my
Emporium on the hill, where the change hums on
wires. Throw away your little bedsocks and your
Welsh wool knitted jacket, I will warm the sheets
like an electric toaster, I will lie by your side like the
Sunday roast...

MISS PRICE
I will knit you a wallet of forget-me-not blue, for
the money to be comfy. I will warm your heart by
the fire so that you can slip it in under your vest
when the shop is closed...

MR EDWARDS
Myfanwy, Myfanwy, before the mice gnaw at your
bottom drawer will you say

MISS PRICE
Yes, Mog, yes, Mog, yes, yes, yes...

MR EDWARDS
And all the bells of the tills of the town shall ring
for our wedding.

[Noise of money-tills and chapel bells.]

Come now, drift up the dark, come up the drifting sea-dark street now in the dark night seesawing like the sea, to the bible-black airless attic over Jack Black the cobbler's shop where alone and savagely Jack Black sleeps in a nightshirt tied to his ankles with elastic and dreams of
chasing the naughty couples down the grassgreen gooseberried double bed of the wood, flogging the tosspots in the spit-and-sawdust, driving out the bare, bold girls from the sixpenny hops of his nightmares...

JACK BLACK [Loudly]

Ach y fi!
Ach y fi!

Evans the Death, the undertaker,

EVANS THE DEATH

laughs high and aloud in his sleep and curls up his toes as he sees, upon waking fifty years ago, snow lie deep on the goosefield behind the sleeping house; and he runs out into the field where his mother is making Welshcakes in the snow, and steals a fistfull of snowflakes and currants and climbs back to bed to eat them cold and sweet under the warm, white clothes while his mother dances in the snow kitchen crying out for her lost currants.

And in the little pink-eyed cottage next to the undertaker's, lie, alone, the seventeen snoring gentle stone of Mister Waldo, rabbitcatcher, barber, herbalist, catdoctor, quack, his fat, pink hands, palms up, over the edge of the patchwork quilt, his black boots neat and tidy in the washing basin, his bowler on a nail above the bed, a milk stout and a slice of cold bread pudding under the pillow; and, dripping in the dark, he dreams of

MOTHER

This little piggy went to market
This little piggy stayed at home
This little piggy had roast beef
This little piggy had none
And this little piggy went

LITTLE BOY
wee wee wee wee wee

MOTHER
all the way home to

WIFE [Screaming]
Waldo! Wal-do!

MR WALDO
Yes, Blodwen love?

WIFE
Oh, what'll the neighbours say, what'll the neighbours...

FIRST NEIGHBOUR
Poor Mrs Waldo

SECOND NEIGHBOUR
What she puts up with

FIRST NEIGHBOUR
Never should of married

SECOND NEIGHBOUR
If she didn't had to

FIRST NEIGHBOUR
Same as her mother.

SECOND NEIGHBOUR
There's a husband for you

FIRST NEIGHBOUR
Bad as his father

SECOND NEIGHBOUR
And you know where he ended

FIRST NEIGHBOUR
Up in the asylum

SECOND NEIGHBOUR
Crying for his ma.

FIRST NEIGHBOUR
Every Saturday

SECOND NEIGHBOUR
He hasn't got a leg

FIRST NEIGHBOUR
And carrying on

SECOND NEIGHBOUR
With that Mrs Beattie Morris

FIRST NEIGHBOUR
Up in the quarry

SECOND NEIGHBOUR
And seen her baby

FIRST NEIGHBOUR
It's got his nose.

SECOND NEIGHBOUR
Oh, it makes my heart bleed

FIRST NEIGHBOUR
What he'll do for drink

SECOND NEIGHBOUR
He sold the pianola

FIRST NEIGHBOUR
And her sewing machine

SECOND NEIGHBOUR
Falling in the gutter

FIRST NEIGHBOUR
Talking to the lamp-post

SECOND NEIGHBOUR
Using language

FIRST NEIGHBOUR
Singing in the w.

SECOND NEIGHBOUR
Poor Mrs Waldo.

WIFE [Tearfully]
Oh, Waldo, Waldo!

MR WALDO
Hush, love, hush. I'm widower Waldo now.

MOTHER [Screaming]
Waldo, Wal-do!

LITTLE BOY
Yes, our mum?

MOTHER
Oh, what'll the neighbours say, what'll the neighbours...

THIRD NEIGHBOUR
Black as a chimbley

FOURTH NEIGHBOUR
Ringing doorbells

THIRD NEIGHBOUR
Breaking windows

FOURTH NEIGHBOUR
Making mudpies

THIRD NEIGHBOUR
Stealing currants

FOURTH NEIGHBOUR
Chalking words

THIRD NEIGHBOUR
Saw him in the bushes

FOURTH NEIGHBOUR
Playing moochins

THIRD NEIGHBOUR
Send him to bed without any supper

FOURTH NEIGHBOUR
Give him sennapods and lock him in the dark

THIRD NEIGHBOUR
Off to the reformatory

FOURTH NEIGHBOUR
Off to the reformatory

TOGETHER
Learn him with a slipper on his b.t.m.

ANOTHER MOTHER [Screaming]
Waldo, Wal-do! what you doing with our Matti?

LITTLE BOY
Give us a kiss, Matti Richards.

LITTLE GIRL
Give us a penny then.

MR WALDO
I only got a halfpenny.

FIRST WOMAN
Lips is a penny.

PREACHER
Will you take this woman Matti Richards

SECOND WOMAN
Dulcie Prothero

THIRD WOMAN
Effie Bevan

FOURTH WOMAN
Lil the Gluepot

FIFTH WOMAN
Mrs Flusher

WIFE
Blodwen Bowen

PREACHER
to be your awful wedded wife

LITTLE BOY [Screaming]
No, no, no!

Now, in her iceberg-white, holily laundered crinoline nightgown, under virtuous polar sheets, in her spruced and scoured dust-defying bedroom in trig and trim Bay View, a house for paying guests, at the top of the town, Mrs Ogmore-Pritchard, widow, twice, of Mr Ogmore, linoleum, retired, and Mr Pritchard, failed bookmaker, who, maddened by besoming, swabbing and scrubbing, the voice of the vacuum-cleaner

and the fume of polish, ironically swallowed disinfectant, fidgets in her
rinsed sleep, wakes in a dream, and nudges in the ribs dead Mr Ogmore,
dead Mr Pritchard, ghostly on either side.

MRS OGMORE-PRITCHARD

Mr Ogmore!
Mr Pritchard!
It is time to inhale your balsam.

MR OGMORE

Oh, Mrs Ogmore!

MR PRITCHARD

Oh, Mrs Pritchard!

MRS OGMORE-PRITCHARD

Soon it will be time to get up.
Tell me your tasks, in order.

MR OGMORE

I must put my pyjamas in the drawer marked
pyjamas.

MR PRITCHARD

I must take my cold bath which is good for me.

MR OGMORE

I must wear my flannel band to ward off sciatica.

MR PRITCHARD

I must dress behind the curtain and put on my
apron.

MR OGMORE

I must blow my nose

MRS OGMORE-PRITCHARD

in the garden, if you please

MR OGMORE

in a piece of tissue-paper which I afterwards burn.

MR PRITCHARD

I must take my salts which are nature's friend.

MR OGMORE

I must boil the drinking water because of germs.

MR PRITCHARD

I must make my herb tea which is free from tannin

MR OGMORE

and have a charcoal biscuit which is good for me.

MR PRITCHARD

I may smoke one pipe of asthma mixture

MRS OGMORE-PRITCHARD

in the woodshed, if you please

MR PRITCHARD

and dust the parlour and spray the canary.

MR OGMORE

I must put on rubber gloves and search the peke for fleas.

MR PRITCHARD

I must dust the blinds and then I must raise them.

MRS OGMORE-PRITCHARD

And before you let the sun in, mind it wipes its shoes.

In Butcher Beynon's, Gossamer Beynon, daughter, schoolteacher, dreaming deep, daintily ferrets under a fluttering hummock of chicken's feathers in a slaughterhouse that has chintz curtains and a three-piece suite, and finds, with no surprise, a small rough ready man with a bushy tail winking in a paper carrier.

ORGAN MORGAN

Help,

cries Organ Morgan, the organist, in his dream,

there is perturbation and music in Coronation Street! All the spouses are honking like geese and the babies singing opera. P.C. Atilla Rees has got his truncheon out and is playing cadenzas by the pump, the cows from Sunday Meadow ring like reindeer, and on the roof of Handel Villa see the Women's Welfare hoofing, bloomered, in the moon.

GOSSAMER BEYNON
At last, my love,

sighs Gossamer Beynon. And the bushy tail wags rude and ginger.

At the sea-end of town, Mr and Mrs Floyd, the cocklers, are sleeping as quiet as death, side by wrinkled side, toothless, salt, and brown, like two old kippers in a box.
And high above, in Salt Lake Farm, Mr Utah Watkins counts, all night, the wife-faced sheep as they leap the fences on the hill, smiling and knitting and bleating just like Mrs Utah Watkins.

UTAH WATKINS [Yawning]
Thirty four, thirty five, thirty six, forty eight, eighty nine...

MRS UTAH WATKINS
Knit one slip one
Knit two together
Pass the slipstich over...
[Mrs Utah Watkins bleats.]

Ocky Milkman, drowned asleep in Cockle Street, is emptying his churns into the Dewi River,

OCKY MILKMAN [Whispering]
regardless of expense,

and weeping like a funeral.

Cherry Owen, next door, lifts a tankard to his lips but nothing flows out of it. He shakes the tankard. It turns into a fish. He drinks the fish. P.C. Atilla Rees

ATILLA REES
lumps out of bed, dead to the dark, and still fog-horning, and drags out his helmet from under the bed; but deep in the backyard lock-up of his sleep a mean voice murmurs,

A VOICE [Murmuring]
You'll be sorry for this in the morning,

ATILLA REES
and he heave-ho's back to bed.

His helmet swashes in the dark.

Willy Nilly, postman, asleep up street, walks fourteen miles to deliver the post as he does every day of the night, and rat-a-tats hard and sharp on Mrs Willy Nilly.

MRS WILLY NILLY
Don't spank me, please, teacher,

whimpers his wife at his side, but every night of her married life she has been late for school.

Sinbad Sailors, over the taproom of the Sailors' Arms, hugs his damp pillow whose secret name is Gossamer Beynon.

A mogul catches Lily Smalls in the wash-house.

LILY SMALLS
Ooh, you old mogul!

Mrs Rose-Cottage's eldest, Mae, peels off her pink-and-white skin in a furnace in a tower in a cave in a waterfall in a wood and waits there raw as an onion for Mister Right to leap up the burning tall hollow splashes of leaves like a brilliantined trout.

MAE ROSE-COTTAGE
[Very close and softly, drawing out the words.]
Call me Dolores
Like they do in the stories.

Alone until she dies, Bessie Bighead, hired help, born in the workhouse, smelling of the cowshed, snores bass and gruff on a couch of straw in a loft in Salt Lake Farm and picks a posy of daisies in Sunday Meadow to put on the grave of Gomer Owen who kissed her once by the pig-sty when she wasn't looking and never kissed her again although she was looking all the time.

And the Inspectors of Cruelty fly down into Mrs Butcher Beynon's dream to persecute Mr Beynon for selling

BUTCHER BEYNON
owl meat, dogs' eyes, manchop.

Mr Beynon, in butcher's bloodied apron, springheels down Coronation Street, a finger, not his own, in his mouth. Straightfaced in his cunning sleep he pulls the legs of his dreams and

BUTCHER BEYNON
hunting on pigback shoots down the wild giblets.

ORGAN MORGAN [High and softly]
Help!

GOSSAMER BEYNON [Softly]
my foxy darling.

Now behind the eyes and secrets of the dreamers in the streets rocked to sleep by the sea, see the titbits and topsyturvies, bobs and buttontops, bags and bones, ash and rind and dandruff and nailparings, saliva and snowflakes and moulted feathers of dreams, the wrecks and sprats and shells and fishbones, whalejuice and moonshine and small salt fry dished up by the hidden sea ...
The owls are hunting. Look, over Bethesda gravestones one hoots and swoops and catches a mouse by Hannah Rees, Belovèd Wife. And in Coronation Street, which you alone can see it is so dark under the chapel in the skies, the Reverend Eli Jenkins, poet, preacher, turns in his deep towards-dawn sleep and dreams of

REV. ELI JENKINS
Eisteddfodau.

He intricately rhymes, to the music of crwth and pibgorn, all night long in his druid's seedy nightie in a beer-tent black with parchs.

Mr Pugh, schoolmaster, fast asleep, pretends to be sleeping, spies foxy round the droop of his nightcap and

MR PUGH
Pssst!

whistles up

Murder.

Mrs Organ Morgan, groceress, coiled grey like a dormouse, her paws to her ears, conjures

MRS ORGAN MORGAN
Silence.

She sleeps very dulcet in a cove of wool, and trumpeting Organ Morgan at her side snores no louder than a spider.
Mary Ann the Sailors dreams of

MARY ANN THE SAILORS
The Garden of Eden.

She comes in her smock-frock and clogs

MARY ANN THE SAILORS
away from the cool scrubbed cobbled kitchen with
the Sunday-school pictures on the whitewashed wall
and the farmers' almanac hung above the settle and
the sides of bacon on the ceiling hooks, and goes
down the cockleshelled paths of that applepie
kitchen garden, ducking under the gippo's clothespegs, catching her apron on the blackcurrant
bushes, past beanrows and onion-bed and tomatoes
ripening on the wall towards the old man playing
the harmonium in the orchard, and sits down on
the grass at his side and shells the green peas that
grow up through the lap of her frock that brushes
the dew.

*In Donkey Street, so furred with sleep, Dai Bread, Polly Garter,
Nogood Boyo, and Lord Cut-Glass sigh before the dawn that is about
to be and dream of*

DAI BREAD
Turkish girls. Horizontal.

POLLY GARTER
Babies.

NOGOOD BOYO
Nothing.

LORD CUT-GLASS
Tick tock tick tock tick tock tick tock.

*Time passes. Listen. Time passes.
An owl flies home past Bethesda, to a chapel in an oak.
And the dawn inches up.*
        [One distant bell-note, faintly reverberating on.]

*Stand on this hill. This is Llareggub Hill, old as the hills, high, cool,
and green, and from this small circle of stones, made not by druids but
by Mrs Beynon's Billy, you can see all the town below you sleeping in
the first of the dawn.*

You can hear the love-sick woodpigeons mooning in bed. A dog barks in his sleep, farmyards away. The town ripples like a lake in the waking haze.

VOICE OF A GUIDE-BOOK

Less than five hundred souls inhabit the three quaint streets and the few narrow bylanes and scattered farmsteads that constitute this small, decaying watering-place which may, indeed, be called a 'backwater of life' without disrespect to its natives who possess, to this day, a salty individuality of their own. The main street, Coronation Street, consists, for the most part, of humble, two-storied houses many of which attempt to achieve some measure of gaiety by prinking themselves out in crude colours and by the liberal use of pinkwash, though there are remaining a few eighteenth-century houses of more pretension, if, on the whole, in a sad state of disrepair. Though there is little to attract the hillclimber, the healthseeker, the sportsman, or the weekending motorist, the contemplative may, if sufficiently attracted to spare it some leisurely hours, find, in its cobbled streets and its little fishing harbour, in its several curious customs, and in the conversation of its local 'characters,' some of that picturesque sense of the past so frequently lacking in towns and villages which have kept more abreast of the times. The river Dewi is said to abound in trout, but is much poached. The one place of worship, with its neglected graveyard, is of no architectural interest.

[A cock crows.]

The principality of the sky lightens now, over our green hill, into spring morning larked and crowed and belling.

[Slow bell notes.]

Who pulls the townhall bellrope but blind Captain Cat? One by one, the sleepers are rung out of sleep this one morning as every morning. And soon you shall see the chimneys' slow upflying snow as Captain

Cat, in sailor's cap and seaboots, announces today with his loud get-out-of-bed bell.

The Reverend Eli Jenkins, in Bethesda House, gropes out of bed into his preacher's black, combs back his bard's white hair, forgets to wash, pads barefoot downstairs, opens the front door, stands in the doorway and, looking out at the day and up at the eternal hill, and hearing the sea break and the gab of birds, remembers his own verses and tells them, softly, to empty Coronation Street that is rising and raising its blinds.

REV. ELI JENKINS

Dear Gwalia! I know there are
Towns lovelier than ours,
And fairer hills and loftier far,
And groves more full of flowers,

And boskier woods more blithe with spring
And bright with birds' adorning,
And sweeter bards than I to sing
Their praise this beauteous morning.

By Cader Idris, tempest-torn,
Or Moel y Wyddfa's glory,
Carnedd Llewelyn beauty born,
Plinlimmon old in story,

By mountains where King Arthur dreams,
By Penmaen Mawr defiant,
Llareggub Hill a molehill seems,
A pygmy to a giant.

By Sawdde, Senni, Dovey, Dee,
Edw, Eden, Aled, all,
Taff and Towy broad and free,
Llyfnant with its waterfall,

Claerwen, Cleddau, Dulas, Daw,
Ely, Gwili, Ogwr, Nedd,
Small is our *River Dewi*, Lord,
A baby on a rushy bed.

By Carreg Cennen, King of time,
Our *Heron Head* is only
A bit of stone with seaweed spread
Where gulls come to be lonely.

A tiny dingle is *Milk Wood*
By golden Grove 'neath Grongar,
But let me choose and oh! I should
Love all my life and longer

To stroll among our trees and stray
In Goosegog Lane, on Donkey Down,
And hear the Dewi sing all day,
And never, never leave the town.

The Reverend Jenkins closes the front door. His morning service is over.

[Slow bell notes.]

Now, woken at last by the out-of-bed-sleepy-head-Polly-put-the-kettle-on townhall bell, Lily Smalls, Mrs Beynon's treasure, comes down-stairs from a dream of royalty who all night long went larking with her full of sauce in the Milk Wood dark, and puts the kettle on the primus ring in Mrs Beynon's kitchen, and looks at herself in Mr Beynon's shaving-glass over the sink, and sees:

LILY SMALLS
Oh, there's a face!
Where you get that hair from?
Got it from a old tom cat.
Give it back then, love.
Oh, there's a perm!

Where you get that nose from, Lily?
Got it from my father, silly.
You've got it on upside down!
Oh, there's a conk!

Look at your complexion!
Oh, no, *you* look.
Needs a bit of make-up.
Needs a veil.
Oh, there's glamour!

Where you get that smile, Lil?
Never you mind, girl.
Nobody loves you.
That's what *you* think.

Who is it loves you?

Shan't tell.
Come on, Lily.
Cross your heart, then?
Cross my heart.

And very softly, her lips almost touching her reflection, she breathes the name and clouds the shaving-glass.

MRS BEYNON [Loudly, from above]

Lily!

LILY SMALLS [Loudly]

Yes, mum...

MRS BEYNON

Where's my tea, girl?

LILY SMALLS

[Softly] Where d'you think? In the cat-box?
[Loudly] Coming up, mum...

Mr Pugh, in the School House opposite, takes up the morning tea to Mrs Pugh, and whispers on the stairs:

MR PUGH

Here's your arsenic, dear.
And your weedkiller biscuit.
I've throttled your parakeet.
I've spat in the vases.
I've put cheese in the mouseholes.
Here's your...
                    [Door creaks open]
   ... nice tea, dear.

MRS PUGH

Too much sugar.

MR PUGH

You haven't tasted it yet, dear.

MRS PUGH

Too much milk, then. Has Mr Jenkins said his poetry?

MR PUGH

Yes, dear.

MRS PUGH
Then it's time to get up. Give me my glasses. No,
not my *reading* glasses, I want to look *out*. I want
to see

Lily Smalls the treasure down on her red knees washing the front step.

She's tucked her dress in her bloomers – oh, the
baggage!

*P.C. Atilla Rees, ox-broad, barge-booted, stomping out of Handcuff
House in a heavy beef-red huff, black-browed under his damp helmet...*

He's going to arrest Polly Garter, mark my words.

MR PUGH
What for, my dear?

MRS PUGH
For having babies.

*... and lumbering down towards the strand to see that the sea is still
there.*
*Mary Ann the Sailors, opening her bedroom window above the
taproom and calling out to the heavens:*

MARY ANN THE SAILORS
I'm eighty five years three months and a day!

MRS PUGH
I will say this for her, she never makes a mistake.

*Organ Morgan at his bedroom window playing chords on the sill to
the morning fishwife gulls who, heckling over Donkey Street, observe:*

DAI BREAD
Me, Dai Bread, hurrying to the bakery, pushing in
my shirt-tails, buttoning my waistcoat, ping goes a
button, why can't they sew them, no time for breakfast, nothing for breakfast, there's wives for you...

MRS DAI BREAD ONE
Me, Mrs Dai Bread One, capped and shawled and
no old corset, nice to be comfy, nice to be nice,
clogging on the cobbles to stir up a neighbour. Oh,
Mrs Sarah, can you spare a loaf, love? Dai Bread

forgot the bread. There's a lovely morning! How's your boils this morning? Isn't that good news now, it's a change to sit down. Ta, Mrs Sarah.

MRS DAI BREAD TWO

Me, Mrs Dai Bread Two, gypsied to kill in a silky scarlet petticoat above my knees, dirty pretty knees, see my body through my petticoat brown as a berry, high heel shoes with one heel missing, tortoiseshell comb in my bright black slinky hair, nothing else at all on but a dab of scent, lolling gaudy at the doorway, tell your fortune in the tea-leaves, scowling at the sunshine, lighting up my pipe.

LORD CUT-GLASS

Me, Lord Cut-Glass, in an old frock-coat belonged to Eli Jenkins and a pair of postman's trousers from Bethesda Jumble, running out of doors to empty slops – mind there, Rover! – and then running in again, tick tock.

NOGOOD BOYO

Me, Nogood Boyo, up to no good in the wash-house.

MISS PRICE

Me, Miss Price, in my pretty print housecoat, deft at the clothesline, natty as a jenny-wren, then pit-pat back to my egg in its cosy, my crisp toast-fingers, my homemade plum and butterpat.

POLLY GARTER

Me, Polly Garter, under the washing line, giving the breast in the garden to my bonny new baby. Nothing grows in our garden, only washing. And babies. And where's their fathers live, my love? Over the hills and far away. You're looking up at me now. I know what you're thinking, you poor little milky creature. You're thinking, you're no better than you should be, Polly, and that's good enough for me. Oh, isn't life a terrible thing, thank God?

[Single long note held by Welsh male voices.]

Now frying-pans spit, kettles and cats purr in the kitchens. The town

smells of seaweed and breakfast all the way down from Bay View, where
Mrs Ogmore-Pritchard, in smock and turban, big-besomed to engage
the dust, picks at her starchless bread and sips lemonrind tea, to Bottom
Cottage, where Mr Waldo, in bowler and bib, gobbles his bubble-and-
squeak and kippers and swigs from the saucebottle. Mary Ann the Sailors

MARY ANN THE SAILORS
praises the Lord who made porridge.

Mr Pugh

MR PUGH
remembers ground glass as he juggles his omelette.

Mrs Pugh

MRS PUGH
nags the salt-cellar.

Willy Nilly postman

WILLY NILLY
downs his last bucket of black brackish tea and
rumbles out bandy to the clucking back where the
hens twitch and grieve for their tea-soaked sops.

Mrs Willy Nilly

MRS WILLY NILLY
full of tea to her double-chinned brim broods and
bubbles over her coven of kettles on the hissing hot
range always ready to steam open the mail.

The Reverend Eli Jenkins

REV. ELI JENKINS
finds a rhyme and dips his pen in his cocoa.

Lord Cut-Glass in his ticking kitchen

LORD CUT-GLASS
scampers from clock to clock, a bunch of clock-keys
in one hand, a fish-head in the other.

Captain Cat in his galley

CAPTAIN CAT
blind and fine-fingered savours his sea-fry.

Mr and Mrs Cherry Owen, in their Donkey Street room that is bedroom, parlour, kitchen, and scullery, sit down to last night's supper of onions boiled in their overcoats and broth of spuds and baconrind and leeks and bones.

MRS CHERRY OWEN

See that smudge on the wall by the picture of Auntie Blossom? That's where you threw the sago.
[Cherry Owen laughs with delight.]
You only missed me by a inch.

CHERRY OWEN

I always miss Auntie Blossom too.

MRS CHERRY OWEN

Remember last night? In you reeled, my boy, as drunk as a deacon with a big wet bucket and a fish-frail full of stout and you looked at me and you said, 'God has come home!' you said, and then over the bucket you went, sprawling and bawling, and the floor was all flagons and eels.

CHERRY OWEN

Was I wounded?

MRS CHERRY OWEN

And then you took off your trousers and you said, 'Does anybody want a fight?' Oh, you old baboon.

CHERRY OWEN

Give us a kiss.

MRS CHERRY OWEN

And then you sang 'Aberystwyth', tenor *and* bass.

CHERRY OWEN

I *always* sing 'Aberystwyth'.

MRS CHERRY OWEN

And then you did a little dance on the table.

CHERRY OWEN

I did?

MRS CHERRY OWEN

Drop dead!

CHERRY OWEN
And then what did I do?

MRS CHERRY OWEN
Then you cried like a baby and said you were a poor
drunk orphan with nowhere to go but the grave.

CHERRY OWEN
And what did I do next, my dear?

MRS CHERRY OWEN
Then you danced on the table all over again and
said you were King Solomon Owen and I was your
Mrs Sheba.

CHERRY OWEN [Softly]
And then?

MRS CHERRY OWEN
And then I got you into bed and you breathed all
night like a brewery.
[Mr and Mrs Cherry Owen laugh
delightedly together.]

*From Beynon Butchers in Coronation Street, the smell of fried liver
sidles out with onions on its breath. And listen! In the dark breakfast-
room behind the shop, Mr and Mrs Beynon, waited upon by their
treasure, enjoy, between bites, their everymorning hullabaloo, and Mrs
Beynon slips the gristly bits under the tasselled tablecloth to her fat cat.*

[Cat purrs.]

MRS BEYNON
She likes the liver, Ben.

MR BEYNON
She ought to do, Bess. It's her brother's.

MRS BEYNON [Screaming]
Oh, d'you hear that, Lily?

LILY SMALLS
Yes, mum.

MRS BEYNON
We're eating pusscat.

LILY SMALLS

Yes, mum.

MRS BEYNON

Oh, you cat-butcher!

MR BEYNON

It was doctored, mind.

MRS BEYNON [Hysterical]

What's that got to do with it?

MR BEYNON

Yesterday, we had mole.

MRS BEYNON

Oh, Lily, Lily!

MR BEYNON

Monday, otter. Tuesday, shrews.

[Mrs Beynon screams.]

LILY SMALLS

Go on, Mrs Beynon. He's the biggest liar in town.

MRS BEYNON

Don't you dare say that about Mr Beynon.

LILY SMALLS

Everybody knows it, mum.

MRS BEYNON

Mr Beynon never tells a lie. Do you, Ben?

MR BEYNON

No, Bess. And now I am going out after the corgis,
with my little cleaver.

MRS BEYNON

Oh, Lily, Lily!

Up the street, in the Sailors' Arms, Sinbad Sailors, grandson of Mary Ann the Sailors, draws a pint in the sunlit bar. The ship's clock in the bar says half past eleven. Half past eleven is opening time. The hands of the clock have stayed still at half past eleven for fifty years. It is always opening time in the Sailors' Arms.

SINBAD
Here's to me, Sinbad.

All over the town, babies and old men are cleaned and put into their broken prams and wheeled on to the sunlit cockled cobbles or out into the backyards under the dancing vests, and left. A baby cries.

OLD MAN
I want my pipe and he wants his bottle.

[School bell rings.]

Noses are wiped, heads picked, hair combed, paws scrubbed, ears boxed, and the children shrilled off to school.

[Children's voices, up and out.]

Fishermen grumble to their nets. Nogood Boyo goes out in the dinghy Zanzibar, ships the oars, drifts slowly in the dab-filled bay, and, lying on his back in the unbaled water, among crabs' legs and tangled lines, looks up at the spring sky.

NOGOOD BOYO [Softly, lazily]
I don't know who's up there and I don't care.

He turns his head and looks up at Llareggub Hill, and sees, among green lathered trees, the white houses of the strewn away farms, where farmboys whistle, dogs shout, cows low, but all too far away for him, or you, to hear. And in the town, the shops squeak open. Mr Edwards, in butterfly-collar and straw-hat at the doorway of Manchester House, measures, with his eye, the dawdlers by, for striped flannel shirts and shrouds and flowery blouses, and bellows to himself, in the darkness behind his eye:

MR EDWARDS [whispers]
I love Miss Price.

Syrup is sold in the post-office. A car drives to market, full of fowls and a farmer. Milk churns stand at Coronation Corner like short, silver policemen. And, sitting at the open window of Schooner House, blind Captain Cat hears all the morning of the town. He hears the voices of children and the noise of children's feet on the cobbles.

CAPTAIN CAT [Softly, to himself]
Maggie Richards, Ricky Rhys, Tommy Powell, our

Sal, little Gerwain, Billy Swansea with the dog's voice, one of Mr Waldo's, nasty Humphrey, Jackie with the sniff ... Where's Dicky's Albie? and the boys from Ty-pant? Perhaps they got the rash again.

[A sudden cry among the children's voices.]

Somebody's hit Maggie Richards. Two to one it's Billy Swansea. Never trust a boy who barks.

[A burst of yelping crying.]

Right again! That's Billy.

And the children's voices cry away.

[Postman's rat-a-tat on door. Distant.]

That's Willy Nilly knocking at Bay View. Rat-a-tat, very soft. The knocker's got a kid glove on. Who's sent a letter to Mrs Ogmore-Pritchard?

[Rat-a-tat. Distant again.]

Careful now, she swabs the front glassy. Every step's like a bar of soap. Mind your size twelveses. That old Bessie would beeswax the lawn to make the birds slip.

WILLY NILLY
Morning, Mrs Ogmore-Pritchard.

MRS OGMORE-PRITCHARD
Good morning, postman.

WILLY NILLY
Here's a letter for you with stamped and addressed envelope enclosed, all the way from Builth Wells. A gentleman wants to study birds and can he have accommodation for two weeks and a bath vegetarian.

MRS OGMORE-PRITCHARD
No.

WILLY NILLY [Persuasively]
You wouldn't know he was in the house, Mrs Ogmore-Pritchard. He'd be out in the mornings at

the bang of dawn with his bag of breadcrumbs and his little telescope...

MRS OGMORE-PRITCHARD
And come home at all hours covered with feathers. I don't want persons in my *nice clean* rooms breathing all over the chairs...

WILLY NILLY
Cross my heart, he won't breathe...

MRS OGMORE-PRITCHARD
and putting their feet on my carpets and sneezing on my china and sleeping in my sheets...

WILLY NILLY
He only wants a *single* bed, Mrs Ogmore-Pritchard.

[Door slams.]

CAPTAIN CAT [Softly]
And back she goes to the kitchen, to polish the potatoes.

Captain Cat hears Willy Nilly's feet heavy on the distant cobbles...

One, two, three, four, five ... That's Mrs Rose-Cottage. What's today? Today she gets the letter from her sister in Gorslas. How's the twins' teeth?

He's stopping at School House.

WILLY NILLY
Morning, Mrs Pugh. Mrs Ogmore-Pritchard won't have a gentleman in from Builth Wells because he'll sleep in her sheets, Mrs Rose-Cottage's sister in Gorslas's twins have got to have them out...

MRS PUGH
Give me the parcel.

WILLY NILLY
It's for *Mr* Pugh, Mrs Pugh.

MRS PUGH
Never you mind. What's inside it?

WILLY NILLY

A book called 'Lives of the Great Poisoners'.

CAPTAIN CAT

That's Manchester House.

WILLY NILLY

Morning, Mr Edwards. Very small news. Mrs Ogmore-Pritchard won't have birds in the house, and Mr Pugh's bought a book now on how to do in Mrs Pugh.

MR EDWARDS

Have you got a letter from *her*?

WILLY NILLY

Miss Price loves you with all her heart. Smelling of lavender today. She's down to the last of the elderflower wine but the quince jam's bearing up and she's knitting roses on the doilies. Last week she sold three jars of boiled sweets, pound of humbugs, half a box of jellybabies and six coloured photos of Llareggub. Yours for ever. Then twenty-one X's.

MR EDWARDS

Oh, Willy Nilly, she's a ruby! Here's my letter. Put it into her hands now.

Down the street comes Willy Nilly. And Captain Cat hears other steps approaching.

CAPTAIN CAT

Mr Waldo hurrying to the Sailors' Arms. Pint of stout with an egg in it.
[Softly] There's a letter for him.

WILLY NILLY

It's another paternity summons, Mr Waldo.

The quick footsteps hurry on along the cobbles and up three steps to the Sailors' Arms.

MR WALDO [Calling out]

Quick, Sinbad. Pint of stout. And no egg in.

People are moving now, up and down the cobbled street.

CAPTAIN CAT

All the women are out this morning, in the sun. You can tell it's Spring. There goes Mrs Cherry, you can tell her by her trotters, off she trots new as a daisy. Who's that talking by the pump? Mrs Floyd and Boyo, talking flatfish. What can you talk about flatfish? That's Mrs Dai Bread One, waltzing up the street like a jelly, every time she shakes it's slap slap slap. Who's that? Mrs Butcher Beynon with her pet black cat, it follows her everywhere, miaow and all. There goes Mrs Twenty Three, important, the sun gets up and goes down in her dewlap, when she shuts her eyes, it's night. High heels now, in the morning too, Mrs Rose-Cottage's eldest, Mae, seventeen and never been kissed ho ho, going young and milking under my window to the field with the nannygoats, she reminds me all the way. Can't hear what the women are gabbing round the pump. Same as ever. Who's having a baby, who blacked whose eye, seen Polly Garter giving her belly an airing, there should be a law, seen Mrs Beynon's new mauve jumper it's her old grey jumper dyed, who's dead, who's dying, there's a lovely day, oh the cost of soapflakes!

[Organ music distant.]

Organ Morgan's at it early. You can *tell* it's Spring.

And he hears the noise of milk-cans.

Ocky Milkman on his round. I will say this, his milk's as fresh as the dew. Half dew it is. Snuffle on, Ocky, watering the town.

Somebody's coming. Now the voices round the pump can see somebody coming. Hush, there's a hush! You can tell by the noise of the hush, it's Polly Garter. [Louder] Hullo, Polly, who's there?

POLLY GARTER [Off]

Me, love.

CAPTAIN CAT
That's Polly Garter. [Softly] Hullo, Polly, my love.

Can you hear the dumb goose-hiss of the wives as they huddle and peck or flounce at a waddle away? Who cuddled you when? Which of their gandering hubbies moaned in Milk Wood for your naughty mothering arms and body like a wardrobe, love? Scrub the floors of the Welfare Hall for the Mothers' Union Social Dance, you're one mother won't wriggle her roly poly bum or pat her fat little buttery foot in that wedding-ringed holy tonight though the waltzing breadwinners snatched from the cosy smoke of the Sailors' Arms will grizzle and mope.

[A cock crows.]

CAPTAIN CAT
Too late, cock, too late,

for the town's half over with its morning. The morning's busy as bees.

[Out background organ music.]

There's the clip clop of horses on the sunhoneyed cobbles of the humming streets, hammering of horseshoes, gobble quack and cackle, tomtit twitter from the bird-ounced boughs, braying on Donkey Down. Bread is baking, pigs are grunting, chop goes the butcher, milk churns bell, tills ring, sheep cough, dogs shout, saws sing. Oh, the Spring whinny and morning moo from the clog dancing farms, the gulls' gab and rabble on the boat bobbing river and sea and the cockles bubbling in the sand, scamper of sanderlings, curlew cry, crow caw, pigeon coo, clock strike, bull bellow, and the ragged gabble of the beargarden school as the women scratch and babble in Mrs Organ Morgan's general shop where everything is sold: custard, buckets, henna, rat-traps, shrimp nets, sugar, stamps, confetti, paraffin, hatchets, whistles.

FIRST WOMAN
Mrs Ogmore-Pritchard

SECOND WOMAN
la di da

FIRST WOMAN
got a man in Builth Wells

THIRD WOMAN
and he got a little telescope to look at birds

SECOND WOMAN
Willy Nilly said

THIRD WOMAN
Remember her first husband? He didn't need a telescope

FIRST WOMAN
he looked at them undressing through the keyhole

THIRD WOMAN
and he used to shout Tallyho

SECOND WOMAN
but Mr Ogmore was a proper gentleman

FIRST WOMAN
even though he hanged his collie

THIRD WOMAN
Seen Mrs Butcher Beynon?

SECOND WOMAN
She said Butcher Beynon put dogs in the mincer

FIRST WOMAN
Go on he's pulling her leg

THIRD WOMAN
Now don't you dare tell her that, there's a dear

SECOND WOMAN
or she'll think he's trying to pull it off and eat it –

FOURTH WOMAN
There's a nasty lot live here when you come to think.

FIRST WOMAN
Look at that Nogood Boyo now

SECOND WOMAN
too lazy to wipe his snout

THIRD WOMAN
and going out fishing every day and all he ever
brought back was a Mrs Samuels

FIRST WOMAN
been in the water a week

SECOND WOMAN
And look at Ocky Milkman's wife that nobody's ever seen

FIRST WOMAN
he keeps her in the cupboard with the empties

THIRD WOMAN
and think of Dai Bread with two wives

SECOND WOMAN
one for the daytime one for the night

FOURTH WOMAN
Men are brutes on the quiet

THIRD WOMAN
And how's Organ Morgan, Mrs Morgan

FIRST WOMAN
you look dead beat

SECOND WOMAN
it's organ organ all the time with him

THIRD WOMAN
up every night until midnight playing the organ

MRS ORGAN MORGAN
Oh, I'm a martyr to music.

Outside, the sun springs down on the rough and tumbling town. It runs through the hedges of Goosegog Lane, cuffing the birds to sing. Spring whips green down Cockle Row, and the shells ring out. Llareggub this snip of a morning is wildfruit and warm, the streets, fields, sands and waters springing in the young sun.

Evans the Death presses hard, with black gloves, on the coffin of his breast, in case his heart jumps out.

EVANS THE DEATH [Harsh]
Where's your dignity. Lie down.

Spring stirs Gossamer Beynon schoolmistress like a spoon.

GOSSAMER BEYNON [Tearful]
Oh, what can I do? I'll *never* be refined if I twitch.

Spring this strong morning foams in a flame in Jack Black as he cobbles a high-heeled shoe for Mrs Dai Bread Two the gypsy, but he hammers it sternly out.

JACK BLACK [To a hammer rhythm]
There is *no leg* belonging to the foot that belongs
to this shoe.

The sun and the green breeze ship Captain Cat sea-memory again.

CAPTAIN CAT
No, *I'll* take the mulatto, by God, who's captain
here? Parlez-vous jig jig, Madam?

Mary Ann the Sailors says very softly to herself as she looks out at Llareggub Hill from the bedroom where she was born,

MARY ANN THE SAILORS [Loudly]
It is Spring in Llareggub in the sun in my old age,
and this is the Chosen Land.

[A choir of children's voices suddenly cries out
on one, high, glad, long, sighing note.]

And in Willy Nilly the Postman's dark and sizzling damp tea-coated misty pygmy kitchen where the spittingcat kettles throb and hop on the range, Mrs Willy Nilly steams open Mr Mog Edwards' letter to Miss Myfanwy Price and reads it aloud to Willy Nilly by the squint of the Spring sun through the one sealed window running with tears, while the drugged, bedraggled hens at the back door whimper and snivel for the lickerish bog-black tea.

MRS WILLY NILLY
From Manchester House, Llareggub. Sole Prop: Mr
Mog Edwards (late of Twll), Linendraper, Hab-
erdasher, Master Tailor, Costumier. For West End
Negligee, Lingerie, Teagowns, Evening Dress,
Trousseaux, Layettes. Also Ready to Wear for All
Occasions. Economical Outfitting for Agricultural
Employment Our Speciality. Wardrobes Bought.
Among Our Satisfied Customers Ministers of
Religion and J.P.'s. Fittings by Appointment. Adver-

tising Weekly in the Twll Bugle. Beloved Myfanwy
Price my Bride in Heaven,

MOG EDWARDS

I love you until Death do us part and then we
shall be together for ever and ever. A new parcel of
ribbons has come from Carmarthen today all the
colours in the rainbow. I wish I could tie a ribbon
in your hair a white one but it cannot be. I dreamed
last night you were all dripping wet and you sat on
my lap as the Reverend Jenkins went down the
street. I see you got a mermaid in your lap he said
and he lifted his hat. He is a proper Christian. Not
like Cherry Owen who said you should have thrown
her back he said. Business is very poorly. Polly
Garter bought two garters with roses but she never
got stockings so what is the use I say. Mr Waldo
tried to sell me a woman's nightie outsize he said he
found it and we know where. I sold a packet of pins
to Tom the Sailors to pick his teeth. If this goes on
I shall be in the Workhouse. My heart is in your
bosom and yours is in mine. God be with you always
Myfanwy Price and keep you lovely for me in His
Heavenly Mansion. I must stop now and remain,
Your Eternal, Mog Edwards.

MRS WILLY NILLY

And then a little message with a rubber stamp. Shop
at Mog's!!!

*And Willy Nilly, rumbling, jockeys out again to the three-seated shack
called the House of Commons in the back where the hens weep, and
sees, in sudden Springshine,*

*herring gulls heckling down to the harbour
where the fishermen spit and prop the morning up and eye the fishy sea
smooth to the sea's end as it lulls in blue. Green and gold money, tobacco,
tinned salmon, hats with feathers, pots of fish-paste, warmth for the
winter-to-be, weave and leap in it rich and slippery in the flash and
shapes of fishes through the cold sea-streets. But with blue lazy eyes the
fishermen gaze at that milk-mild whispering water with no ruck or ripple
as though it blew great guns and serpents and typhooned the town.*

FISHERMAN
Too rough for fishing today.

And they thank God, and gob at a gull for luck, and moss-slow and silent make their way uphill, from the still still sea, towards the Sailors' Arms as the children

[School bell.]

spank and scamper rough and singing out of school into the draggletail yard. And Captain Cat at his window says soft to himself the words of their song.

CAPTAIN CAT [Keeping to the beat of the singing]
Johnnie Crack and Flossie Snail
Kept their baby in a milking pail
Flossie Snail and Johnnie Crack
One would pull it out and one would put it back
O it's my turn now said Flossie Snail
To take the baby from the milking pail
And it's my turn now said Johnnie Crack
To smack it on the head and put it back

Johnnie Crack and Flossie Snail
Kept their baby in a milking pail
One would put it back and one would pull it out
And all it had to drink was ale and stout
For Johnnie Crack and Flossie Snail
Always used to say that stout and ale
Was *good* for a baby in a milking pail.

[Pause.]

The music of the spheres is heard distinctly over Milk Wood. It is 'The Rustle of Spring'.
A glee-party sings in Bethesda Graveyard, gay but muffled.
Vegetables make love above the tenors.
And dogs bark blue in the face.
Mrs Ogmore-Pritchard belches in a teeny hanky and chases the sunlight with a flywhisk, but even she cannot drive out the Spring: from one of her fingerbowls, a primrose grows.

Mrs Dai Bread One and Mrs Dai Bread Two are sitting outside their house in Donkey Lane, one darkly one plumply blooming in the quick, dewy sun. Mrs Dai Bread Two is looking into a crystal ball which she holds in the lap of her dirty scarlet petticoat, hard against her hard dark thighs.

MRS DAI BREAD TWO
Cross my palm with silver. Out of our housekeeping money. Aah!

MRS DAI BREAD ONE
What d'you see, lovie?

MRS DAI BREAD TWO
I see a featherbed. With three pillows on it. And a text above the bed. I can't read what it says, there's great clouds blowing. Now they have blown away. God is love, the text says.

MRS DAI BREAD ONE [Delighted]
That's *our* bed.

MRS DAI BREAD TWO
And now it's vanished. The sun's spinning like a top. Who's this coming out of the sun? It's a hairy little man with big pink lips. He got a wall eye.

MRS DAI BREAD ONE
It's Dai, it's Dai Bread!

MRS DAI BREAD TWO
Ssh! The featherbed's floating back. The little man's taking his boots off. He's pulling his shirt over his head. He's beating his chest with his fists. He's climbing into bed.

MRS DAI BREAD ONE
Go on, go on.

MRS DAI BREAD TWO
There's *two* women in bed. He looks at them both, with his head cocked on one side. He's whistling through his teeth. Now he grips his little arms round one of the women.

MRS DAI BREAD ONE
Which one, which one?

MRS DAI BREAD TWO
I can't see any more. There's great clouds blowing
again.

MRS DAI BREAD ONE
Ach, the mean old clouds!

*The morning is all singing. The Reverend Eli Jenkins, busy on his
morning calls, stops outside the Welfare Hall to hear Polly Garter as she
scrubs the floors for the Mothers' Union Dance tonight.*

POLLY GARTER [Singing]
I loved a man whose name was Tom
He was strong as a bear and two yards long
I loved a man whose name was Dick
He was big as a barrel and three feet thick
And I loved a man whose name was Harry
Six feet tall and sweet as a cherry
But the one I loved best awake or asleep
Was little Willy Wee and he's six feet deep.

Oh Tom Dick and Harry were three fine men
And I'll never have such loving again
But little Willy Wee who took me on his knee
Little Willy Weazel is the man for me.

Now men from every parish round
Run after me and roll me on the ground
But whenever I love another man back
Johnnie from the Hill or Sailing Jack
I always think as they do what they please
Of Tom Dick and Harry who were tall as trees
And most I think when I'm by their side
Of little Willy Wee who downed and died.

Oh Tom Dick and Harry were three fine men
And I'll never have such loving again
But little Willy Wee who took me on his knee
Little Willy Weazel is the man for me.

REV. ELI JENKINS
Praise the Lord! We are a musical nation.

*And the Reverend Jenkins hurries on through the town, to visit the
sick with jelly and poems.*

The town's as full as a lovebird's egg.

MR WALDO
There goes the Reverend,

says Mr Waldo at the smoked herring brown window of the unwashed Sailors' Arms

                              with his brolly and
            his odes. Fill 'em up, Sinbad, I'm on the
            treacle today.

The silent fishermen flush down their pints.

SINBAD
Oh, Mr Waldo,

sighs Sinbad Sailors,
                        I dote on that Gossamer Beynon.

Love, sings the Spring. The bedspring grass bounces under birds' bums and lambs.
And Gossamer Beynon, schoolteacher, spoonstirred and quivering, teaches her slubberdegullion class

CHILDREN'S VOICES
It was a luvver and his lars
With a a and a o and a a nonino...

GOSSAMER BEYNON
Naow, naow, naow, your eccents, children!
It was a lover and his less
With a hey and a hao and a hey nonino...

SINBAD
Oh, Mr Waldo,

says Sinbad Sailors,
                        she's a lady all over.

And Mr Waldo, who is thinking of a woman soft as Eve and sharp as sciatica to share his bread-pudding bed, answers,

MR WALDO
No lady that I know is.

SINBAD

And if only grandma'd die, cross my heart I'd go down on my knees Mr Waldo and I'd say Miss Gossamer I'd say

CHILDREN'S VOICES

When birds do sing a ding a ding a ding
Sweet luvvers luv the Spring...

Polly Garter sings, still on her knees,

POLLY GARTER

Tom Dick and Harry were three fine men
And I'll never have such

CHILDREN

Ding a ding

POLLY GARTER

again.

And the morning school is over, and Captain Cat at his curtained schooner's porthole open to the Spring sun tides hears the naughty forfeiting children tumble and rhyme on the cobbles...

GIRLS' VOICES

Gwennie call the boys
They make such a noise.

GIRL

Boys boys boys
Come along to me.

GIRLS' VOICES

Boys boys boys
Kiss Gwennie where she says
Or give her a penny.
Go on, Gwennie.

GIRL

Kiss me in Goosegog Lane
Or give me a penny.
What's your name?

FIRST BOY

Billy.

GIRL

Kiss me in Goosegog Lane Billy
Or give me a penny silly.

FIRST BOY

Gwennie Gwennie
I kiss you in Goosegog Lane
Now I haven't got to give you a penny.

GIRLS' VOICES

Boys boys boys
Kiss Gwennie where she says
Or give her a penny.
Go on, Gwennie.

GIRL

Kiss me on Llareggub Hill.
Or give me a penny
What's your name?

SECOND BOY

Johnnie Cristo.

GIRL

Kiss me on Llareggub Hill Johnnie Cristo
Or give me a penny, mister.

SECOND BOY

Gwennie Gwennie
I kiss you on Llareggub Hill.
Now I haven't got to give you a penny.

GIRLS' VOICES

Boys boys boys
Kiss Gwennie where she says
Or give her a penny.
Go on, Gwennie.

GIRL

Kiss me in Milk Wood
Or give me a penny.
What's your name?

THIRD BOY

Dicky.

GIRL

Kiss me in Milk Wood Dicky
Or give me a penny quickly.

THIRD BOY

Gwennie Gwennie
I can't kiss you in Milk Wood.

GIRLS' VOICES

Gwennie ask him why.

GIRL

Why?

THIRD BOY

Because my mother said I mustn't.

GIRLS' VOICES

Cowardy cowardy custard
Give Gwennie a penny.

GIRL

Give me a penny.

THIRD BOY

I haven't got any.

GIRLS' VOICES

Put him in the river
Up to his liver
Quick quick Dirty Dick
Beat him on the bum
With a rhubarb stick.
Aiee!
Hush!

And the shrill girls giggle and master around him and squeal as they clutch and thrash, and he blubbers away downhill with his patched pants falling, and his tear-splashed blush burns all the way as the triumphant bird-like sisters scream with buttons in their claws and the bully brothers hoot after him his little nickname and his mother's shame and his father's wickedness with the loose wild barefoot women of the hovels of the hills. It all means nothing at all, and, howling for his milky mum, for her cawl and buttermilk and cowbreath and Welshcakes and the fat birth-smelling bed and moonlit kitchen of her arms, he'll never forget as

he paddles blind home through the weeping end of the world. Then his
tormentors tussle and run to the Cockle Street sweet-shop, their pennies
sticky as honey, to buy from Miss Myfanwy Price, who is cocky and neat
as a puff-bosomed robin and her small round buttocks tight as ticks,
gobstoppers big as wens that rainbow as you suck, brandyballs, wine-
gums, hundreds and thousands, liquorice sweet as sick, nugget to tug
and ribbon out like another red rubbery tongue, gum to glue in girls'
curls, crimson coughdrops to spit blood, ice-cream cornets, dandelion-
and-burdock, raspberry and cherryade, pop goes the weasel and the
wind.

Gossamer Beynon high-heels out of school. The sun hums down
through the cotton flowers of her dress into the bell of her heart and
buzzes in the honey there and couches and kisses, lazy-loving and boozed,
in her red-berried breast. Eyes run from the trees and windows of the
street steaming, 'Gossamer', and strip her to the nipples and the bees.
She blazes naked past the Sailors' Arms, the only woman on the Dai-
Adamed earth. Sinbad Sailors places on her thighs still dewdamp from
the first mangrowing cockcrow garden his reverent goat-bearded hands.

GOSSAMER BEYNON
I don't care if he *is* common,

she whispers to her salad-day deep self,

I want to gobble him up.
I don't care if he *does* drop his aitches,

she tells the stripped and mother-of-the-world big-beamed and Eve-
hipped spring of her self,

so long as
he's all cucumber and hooves.

Sinbad Sailors watches her go by, demure and proud and schoolmarm
in her crisp flower dress and sun-defying hat, with never a look or lilt or
wriggle, the butcher's unmelting icemaiden daughter veiled forever from
the hungry hug of his eyes.

SINBAD SAILORS
Oh, Gossamer Beynon, why are you so proud?

He grieves to his Guinness.

Oh, beautiful beautiful Gossamer B., I wish I wish

that you were for me. I wish you were not so edu-
cated.

*She feels his goatbeard tickle her in the middle of the world like a tuft of
wiry fire, and she turns, in a terror of delight, away from his whips and
whiskery conflagration and sits down in the kitchen to a plate heaped
high with chips and the kidneys of lambs.*

*In the blind-drawn dark dining-room of School House, dusty and
echoing as a dining room in a vault, Mr and Mrs Pugh are silent over
cold grey cottage pie. Mr Pugh reads, as he forks the shroud meat in,
from 'Lives of the Great Poisoners'. He has bound a plain brown-paper
cover round the book. Slyly, between slow mouthfuls, he sidespies up at
Mrs Pugh, poisons her with his eye, then goes on reading. He underlines
certain passages and smiles in secret.*

MRS PUGH
Persons with manners do not read at table,

*says Mrs Pugh. She swallows a digestive tablet as big as a horse-pill,
washing it down with clouded peasoup water.*

[Pause.]

Some persons were brought up in pigsties.

MR PUGH
Pigs don't read at table, dear.

*Bitterly she flicks dust from the broken cruet. It settles on the pie in a
thin gnat-rain.*

Pigs can't read, my dear.

MRS PUGH
I know one who can.

*Alone in the hissing laboratory of his wishes, Mr Pugh minces among
bad vats and jeroboams, tiptoes through spinneys of murdering herbs,
agony dancing in his crucibles, and mixes especially for Mrs Pugh a
venomous porridge unknown to toxologists which will scald and viper
through her until her ears fall off like figs, her toes grow big and black
as balloons, and steam comes screaming out of her navel.*

MR PUGH
You know best, dear,

says Mr Pugh, and quick as a flash he ducks her in rat soup.

MRS PUGH

What's that book by your trough, Mr Pugh?

MR PUGH

It's a theological work, my dear. 'Lives of the Great
Saints.'

Mrs Pugh smiles. An icicle forms in the cold air of the dining vault.

MRS PUGH

I saw you talking to a saint this morning. Saint Polly
Garter. She was martyred again last night in Milk
Wood. Mrs Organ Morgan saw her with Mr Waldo.

MRS ORGAN MORGAN

And when they saw me they pretended they were
looking for nests,

*said Mrs Organ Morgan to her husband, with her mouth full of fish as
a pelican's.*

But you don't go nesting in long combinations, I
said to myself, like Mr Waldo was wearing, and
your dress nearly over your head like Polly Garter's.
Oh, they didn't fool me.

*One big bird gulp, and the flounder's gone. She licks her lips and goes
stabbing again.*

And when you think of all those babies she's got,
then all I can say is she'd better give up bird nesting
that's all I can say, it isn't the right kind of hobby at
all for a woman that can't say No even to midgets.
Remember Tom Spit? He wasn't any bigger than a
baby and he gave her two. But they're two nice boys,
I will say that, Fred Spit and Arthur. Sometimes I
like Fred best and sometimes I like Arthur. Who do
you like best, Organ?

ORGAN MORGAN

Oh, Bach without any doubt. Bach every time for
me.

MRS ORGAN MORGAN
Organ Morgan, you haven't been listening to a word
I said. It's organ organ all the time with you...

*And she bursts into tears, and, in the middle of her salty howling, nimbly
spears a small flat fish and pelicans it whole.*

ORGAN MORGAN
And then Palestrina,

says Organ Morgan.

Lord Cut-Glass, in his kitchen full of time, squats down alone to a
dogdish, marked Fido, of peppery fish-scraps and listens to the voices of
his sixty-six clocks – (one for each year of his loony age) – and watches,
with love, their black-and-white moony loudlipped faces tocking the
earth away: slow clocks, quick clocks, pendulumed heart-knocks, china,
alarm, grandfather, cuckoo; clocks shaped like Noah's whirring Ark,
clocks that bicker in marble ships, clocks in the wombs of glass women,
hourglass chimers, tu-wit-tu-woo clocks, clocks that pluck tunes, Vesu-
vius clocks all black bells and lava, Niagara clocks that cataract their
ticks, old time-weeping clocks with ebony beards, clocks with no hands
forever drumming out time without ever knowing what time it is. His
sixty-six singers are all set at different hours. Lord Cut-Glass lives in a
house and a life at siege. Any minute or dark day now, the unknown
enemy will loot and savage downhill, but they will not catch him napping.
Sixty-six different times in his fish-slimy kitchen ping, strike, tick, chime
and tock.

The lust and lilt and lather and emerald breeze and crackle of the bird-
praise and body of Spring with its breasts full of rivering May-milk,
means, to that lordly fish-head nibbler, nothing but another nearness to
the tribes and navies of the Last Black Day who'll sear and pillage down
Armageddon Hill to his double-locked rusty-shuttered tick tock dust-
scrabbled shack at the bottom of the town that has fallen head over bells
in love.

POLLY GARTER
And I'll never have such loving again,

pretty Polly hums and longs.

POLLY GARTER [Sings]
Now when farmers' boys on the first fair day
Come down from the hills to drink and be gay,

Before the sun sinks I'll lie there in their arms –
For they're *good* bad boys from the lonely farms,

But I always think as we tumble into bed
Of little Willy Wee who is dead, dead, dead...

[A long silence.]

The sunny slow lulling afternoon yawns and moons through the dozy town. The sea lolls, laps and idles in, with fishes sleeping in its lap. The meadows still as Sunday, the shut-eye tasselled bulls, the goat-and-daisy dingles, nap happy and lazy. The dumb duck-ponds snooze. Clouds sag and pillow on Llareggub Hill. Pigs grunt in a wet wallow-bath, and smile as they snort and dream. They dream of the acorned swill of the world, the rooting for pig-fruit, the bagpipe dugs of the mother sow, the squeal and snuffle of yesses of the women pigs in rut. They mud-bask and snout in the pig-loving sun; their tails curl; they rollick and slobber and snore to deep, smug, after-swill sleep. Donkeys angelically drowse on Donkey Down.

MRS PUGH
Persons with manners,

snaps Mrs cold Pugh,

do not nod at table.

Mr Pugh cringes awake. He puts on a soft-soaping smile: it is sad and grey under his nicotine-eggyellow weeping walrus Victorian moustache worn thick and long in memory of Doctor Crippen.

You should wait until you retire to your sty,

says Mrs Pugh, sweet as a razor. His fawning measly quarter-smile freezes. Sly and silent, he foxes into his chemist's den and there, in a hiss and prussic circle of cauldrons and phials brimful with pox and the Black Death, cooks up a fricassee of deadly nightshade, nicotine, hot frog, cyanide and bat-spit for his needling stalactite hag and bednag of a pokerbacked nutcracker wife.

MR PUGH
I beg your pardon, my dear,

he murmurs with a wheedle.

Captain Cat, at his window thrown wide to the sun and the clippered seas he sailed long ago when his eyes were blue and bright, slumbers and voyages; ear-ringed and rolling, I Love You Rosie Probert tattooed on his belly, he brawls with broken bottles in the fug and babel of the dark dock bars, roves with a herd of short and good time cows in every naughty port and twines and souses with the drowned and blowsy-breasted dead. He weeps as he sleeps and sails, and the tears run down his grog-blossomed nose.

One voice of all he remembers most dearly as his dream buckets down. Lazy early Rosie with the flaxen thatch, whom he shared with Tom-Fred the donkeyman and many another seaman, clearly and near to him speaks from the bedroom of her dust. In that gulf and haven, fleets by the dozen have anchored for the little heaven of the night; but she speaks to Captain napping Cat alone. Mrs Probert –

ROSIE PROBERT
From Duck Lane, Jack. Quack twice and ask for
Rosie –

is the one love of his sea-life that was sardined with women.

ROSIE PROBERT [Softly]
What seas did you see,
Tom Cat, Tom Cat,
In your sailoring days
Long long ago?
What sea beasts were
In the wavery green
When you were my master?

CAPTAIN CAT
I'll tell you the truth.
Seas barking like seals,
Blue seas and green,
Seas covered with eels
And mermen and whales.

ROSIE PROBERT
What seas did you sail
Old whaler when
On the blubbery waves
Between Frisco and Wales
You were my bosun?

CAPTAIN CAT
As true as I'm here dear
You Tom Cat's tart
You landlubber Rosie
You cosy love
My easy as easy
My true sweetheart,
Seas green as a bean
Seas gliding with swans
In the seal-barking moon.

ROSIE PROBERT
What seas were rocking
My little deck hand
My favourite husband
In your seaboots and hunger
My duck my whaler
My honey my daddy
My pretty sugar sailor
With my name on your belly
When you were a boy
Long long ago?

CAPTAIN CAT
I'll tell you no lies.
The only sea I saw
Was the seesaw sea
With you riding on it.
Lie down, lie easy.
Let me shipwreck in your thighs.

ROSIE PROBERT
Knock twice, Jack,
At the door of my grave
And ask for Rosie.

CAPTAIN CAT
Rosie Probert.

ROSIE PROBERT
Remember her.
She is forgetting.
The earth which filled her mouth

Is vanishing from her.
Remember me.
I have forgotten you.
I am going into the darkness of the darkness for
    ever.
I have forgotten that I was ever born.

CHILD
Look,

*says a child to her mother as they pass by the window of Schooner
House,*

Captain Cat is crying.

Captain Cat is crying,

CAPTAIN CAT
Come back come back,

up the silences and echoes of the passages of the eternal night.

CHILD
He's crying all over his nose,

says the child. Mother and child move on down the street.

He's got a nose like strawberries,

*the child says; and then she forgets him too. She sees in the still middle
of the bluebagged bay Nogood Boyo fishing from the Zanzibar.*

Nogood Boyo gave me three pennies yesterday but
I wouldn't,

the child tells her mother.

Boyo catches a whalebone corset. It is all he
has caught all day.

NOGOOD BOYO
Bloody funny fish!

*Mrs Dai Bread Two gypsies up his mind's slow eye, dressed only in a
bangle.*

She's wearing her nightgown.
[Pleadingly] Would you like this nice wet corset,
Mrs Dai Bread Two?

MRS DAI BREAD TWO
No, I *won't*!

NOGOOD BOYO
And a bite of my little apple?

he offers with no hope.

> *She shakes her brass nightgown, and he chases her out of his mind; and when he comes gusting back, there in the bloodshot centre of his eye a geisha girl grins and bows in a kimono of ricepaper.*

I want to be *good* Boyo, but nobody'll let me,

he sighs as she writhes politely. The land fades, the sea flocks silently away; and through the warm white cloud where he lies silky, tingling uneasy Eastern music undoes him in a Japanese minute.

The afternoon buzzes like lazy bees round the flowers round Mae Rose-Cottage. Nearly asleep in the field of nannygoats who hum and gently butt the sun, she blows love on a puffball.

MAE ROSE-COTTAGE [Lazily]
He loves me
He loves me not
He loves me
He loves me not
He *loves* me! – the dirty old fool.

Lazy she lies alone in clover and sweet-grass, seventeen and never been sweet in the grass, ho ho.

The Reverend Eli Jenkins inky in his cool front parlour or poem-room tells only the truth in his Lifework: the Population, Main Industry, Shipping, History, Topography, Flora and Fauna of the town he worships in: the White Book of Llareggub. Portraits of famous bards and preachers, all fur and wool from the squint to the kneecaps, hang over him heavy as sheep, next to faint lady watercolours of pale green Milk Wood like a lettuce salad dying. His mother, propped against a pot in a palm, with her wedding-ring waist and bust like a blackcloth diningtable, suffers in her stays.

REV. ELI JENKINS
Oh, angels be careful there with your knives and
forks,

he prays. There is no known likeness of his father Esau, who, undog-collared because of his little weakness, was scythed to the bone one harvest by mistake when sleeping with his weakness in the corn. He lost all ambition and died, with one leg.

Poor Dad,

grieved the Reverend Eli,

to die of drink and agriculture.

Farmer Watkins in Salt Lake Farm hates his cattle on the hill as he ho's them in to milking.

UTAH WATKINS [In a fury]
Damn you, you damned dairies!

A cow kisses him.

Bite her to death!

he shouts to his deaf dog who smiles and licks his hand.

Gore him, sit on him, Daisy!

he bawls to the cow who barbed him with her tongue, and she moos gentle words as he raves-and-dances among his summerbreath'd slaves walking delicately to the farm. The coming of the end of the Spring day is already reflected in the lakes of their great eyes. Bessie Bighead greets them by the names she gave them when they were maidens:

BESSIE BIGHEAD
Peg, Meg, Buttercup, Moll,
Fan from the Castle,
Theodosia and Daisy.

They bow their heads.

Look up Bessie Bighead in the White Book of Llareggub and you will find the few haggard rags and the one poor glittering thread of her history laid out in pages there with as much love and care as the lock of hair of a first lost love. Conceived in Milk Wood, born in a barn, wrapped in paper, left on a doorstep, big-headed and bass-voiced she grew in the dark until long-dead Gomer Owen kissed her when she wasn't looking because he was dared. Now in the light she'll work, sing, milk, say the cows' sweet names and sleep until the night sucks out her soul and spits it into the sky. In her life-long love-light, holily Bessie milks the fond lake-eyed cows as dusk showers slowly down over byre, sea and town.

Utah Watkins curses through the farmyard on a carthorse.

UTAH WATKINS

Gallop, you bleeding cripple! –

and the huge horse neighs softly as though he had given it a lump of sugar.

Now the town is dusk. Each cobble, donkey, goose and gooseberry street is a thoroughfare of dusk; and dusk and ceremonial dust, and night's first darkening snow, and the sleep of birds, drift under and through the live dusk of this place of love. Llareggub is the capital of dusk.

Mrs Ogmore-Pritchard, at the first drop of the dusk-shower, seals all her Sea View doors, draws the germ-free blinds, sits, erect as a dry dream on a highbacked hygienic chair and wills herself to cold, quick sleep. At once, at twice, Mr Ogmore and Mr Pritchard, who all dead day long have been gossiping like ghosts in the woodshed, planning the loveless destruction of their glass widow, reluctantly sigh and sidle into her clean house.

MR PRITCHARD

You first, Mr Ogmore.

MR OGMORE

After you, Mr Pritchard.

MR PRITCHARD

No, no, Mr Ogmore. You widowed her first.

And in through the keyhole, with tears where their eyes once were, they ooze and grumble.

MRS OGMORE-PRITCHARD

Husbands,

she says in her sleep. There is acid love in her voice for one of the two shambling phantoms. Mr Ogmore hopes that it is not for him. So does Mr Pritchard.

I love you both.

MR OGMORE [With terror]

Oh, Mrs Ogmore.

MR PRITCHARD [With horror]
Oh, Mrs Pritchard.

MRS OGMORE-PRITCHARD
Soon it will be time to go to bed. Tell me your tasks
in order.

MR OGMORE & MR PRITCHARD
We must take our pyjamas from the drawer marked
pyjamas.

MRS OGMORE-PRITCHARD [Coldly]
And then you must take them off.

*Down in the dusking town, Mae Rose-Cottage, still lying in clover,
listening to the nannygoats chew, draws circles of lipstick round her
nipples.*

MAE ROSE-COTTAGE
I'm *fast*. I'm a bad lot. God will strike me dead. I'm
seventeen. I'll go to hell,

she tells the goats.

You just wait. I'll sin till I blow up!

*She lies deep, waiting for the worst to happen; the goats champ and
sneer.*

*And at the doorway of Bethesda House, the Reverend Jenkins recites
to Llareggub Hill his sunset poem.*

REV. ELI JENKINS
Every morning, when I wake,
Dear Lord, a little prayer I make,
O please to keep Thy lovely eye
On all poor creatures born to die.

And every evening at sun-down
I ask a blessing on the town,
For whether we last the night or no
I'm sure is always touch-and-go.

We are not wholly bad or good
Who live our lives under Milk Wood,
And Thou, I know, wilt be the first
To see our best side, not our worst.

O let us see another day!
Bless us this holy night, I pray,
And to the sun we all will bow
And say goodbye – but just for now!

Jack Black prepares once more to meet his Satan in the Wood. He grinds his night-teeth, closes his eyes, climbs into his religious trousers, their flies sewn up with cobbler's thread, and pads out, torched and bibled, grimly, joyfully, into the already sinning dusk.

JACK BLACK
Off to Gomorrah!

And Lily Smalls is up to Nogood Boyo in the wash-house.
Cherry Owen, sober as Sunday as he is every day of the week, goes off happy as Saturday to get drunk as a deacon as he does every night.

CHERRY OWEN
I always say she's got two husbands,

says Cherry Owen,

one drunk

and one sober.

And Mrs Cherry simply says

MRS CHERRY OWEN
And aren't I a lucky woman? Because I love them both.

SINBAD
Evening, Cherry.

CHERRY OWEN
Evening, Sinbad.

SINBAD
What'll you have?

CHERRY OWEN
Too much.

SINBAD
The *Sailors'* Arms is always open,

Sinbad suffers to himself, heartbroken,

                                    Oh, Gossamer,
            open yours!

*Dusk is drowned for ever until tomorrow. It is all at once night now.
The windy town is a hill of windows, and from the larrupped waves, the
lights of the lamps in the windows call back the day and the dead that
have run away to sea. All over the calling dark, babies and old men are
bribed and lullabied to sleep.*

                    FIRST WOMAN'S VOICE
            Hushabye, baby, the sandman is coming...

                    SECOND WOMAN'S VOICE
            Rockabye, grandpa, in the treetop,
            When the wind blows, the cradle will rock,
            When the bough breaks, the cradle will fall,
            Down will come grandpa, whiskers and all.

*Or their daughters cover up the old unwinking men like parrots, and
in their little dark in the lit and bustling young kitchen corners, all night
long they watch, beady-eyed, the long night through in case death catches
them asleep.*

*Unmarried girls, alone in their privately bridal bedrooms, powder and
curl for the Dance of the World.*

                    [Accordion music – dim.]

*They make, in front of their looking-glasses, haughty or come-hithering
faces for the young men in the street outside, at the lamplit leaning
corners, who wait in the all-at-once wind to wolve and whistle.*

            [Accordion music up and down and continuing dim.]

The drinkers in the Sailors' Arms drink to the failure of the dance.

                    FIRST DRINKER
            Down with the waltzing and skipping.

                    SECOND DRINKER
            Dancing isn't natural,

*righteously says Cherry Owen who has just downed seventeen pints of
flat, warm, thin, Welsh, bitter beer.*

A farmer's lantern glimmers, a spark on Llareggub hillside.

Llareggub Hill, writes the Reverend Jenkins in his poem-room, that mystic tumulus, the memorial of peoples that dwelt in the region of Llareggub before the Celts left the Land of Summer and where the old wizards made themselves a wife out of flowers.

[Accordion music out.]

Mr Waldo, in his corner of the Sailors' Arms, sings:

MR WALDO

In Pembroke City when I was young
I lived by the Castle Keep
Sixpence a week was my wages
For working for the chimbley sweep.

Six cold pennies he gave me
Not a farthing more or less
And all the fare I could afford
Was parsnip gin and watercress.

I did not need a knife and fork
Or a bib up to my chin
To dine on a dish of watercress
And a jug of parsnip gin.

Did you ever hear a growing boy
To live so cruel cheap
On grub that has no flesh and bones
And liquor that makes you weep?

Sweep sweep chimbley sweep,
I wept through Pembroke City
Poor and barefoot in the snow
Till a kind young woman took pity.

Poor little chimbley sweep she said
Black as the ace of spades
Oh nobody's swept my chimbley
Since my husband went his ways.

Come and sweep my chimbley
Come and sweep my chimbley
She sighed to me with a blush
Come and sweep my chimbley
Come and sweep my chimbley
Bring along your chimbley brush!

Blind Captain Cat climbs into his bunk. Like a cat, he sees in the dark. Through the voyages of his tears, he sails to see the dead.

CAPTAIN CAT
Dancing Williams!

FIRST DROWNED
Still dancing.

CAPTAIN CAT
Jonah Jarvis

THIRD DROWNED
Still.

Curly Bevan's skull.

ROSIE PROBERT
Rosie, with God. She has forgotten dying.

The dead come out in their Sunday best.
Listen to the night breaking.
Organ Morgan goes to chapel to play the organ. He plays alone at night to anyone who will listen: lovers, revellers, the silent dead, tramps or sheep. He sees Bach lying on a tombstone.

ORGAN MORGAN
Johann Sebastian!

CHERRY OWEN [Drunkenly]
Who?

ORGAN MORGAN
Johann Sebastian mighty Bach. Oh, Bach, fach.

CHERRY OWEN
To hell with you,

says Cherry Owen who is resting on the tombstone on his way home.
Mr Mog Edwards and Miss Myfanwy Price happily apart from one another at the top and the sea-end of the town write their everynight letters of love and desire. In the warm White Book of Llareggub you will find the little maps of the islands of their contentment.

MYFANWY PRICE
Oh, my Mog, I am yours for ever.

And she looks around with pleasure at her own neat neverdull room which Mr Mog Edwards will never enter.

MOG EDWARDS
Come to my arms, Myfanwy.

And he hugs his lovely money to his own heart.

And Mr Waldo drunk in Milk Wood hugs his lovely Polly Garter under the eyes and rattling tongues of the neighbours and the birds, and he does not care. He smacks his live red lips.

But it is not his name that Polly Garter whispers as she lies under the oak and loves him back. Six feet deep that name sings in the cold earth.

POLLY GARTER [Sings]
But I always think as we tumble into bed
Of little Willy Wee who is dead, dead, dead.

The thin night darkens. A breeze from the creased water sighs the streets close under Milk waking Wood. The Wood, whose every tree-foot's cloven in the black glad sight of the hunters of lovers, that is a God-built garden to Mary Ann the Sailors who knows there is Heaven on earth and the chosen people of His kind fire in Llareggub's land, that is the fairday farmhands' wantoning ignorant chapel of bridebeds, and, to the Reverend Eli Jenkins, a greenleaved sermon on the innocence of men, the suddenly wind-shaken wood springs awake for the second dark time this one Spring day.

EXPLANATORY NOTES

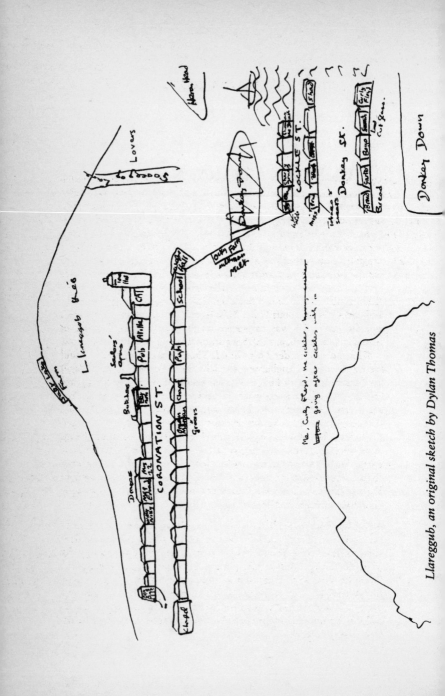

Llareggub, an original sketch by Dylan Thomas

EXPLANATORY NOTES

Under Milk Wood (title):   After a period in which Thomas referred to the work under various forms of the title 'The Town That Was Mad' (see Introduction), the working title became 'Llareggub Hill' (abbreviated to 'Llareggub' when the first half was published in *Botteghe Oscure* in April 1952). John Malcolm Brinnin records a conversation with Thomas in Laugharne in September 1952: 'When I suggested that perhaps he might find a better title than *Llareggub Hill* for his "play for voices", he agreed at once. The joke in the present title was a small and childish one, he felt; beyond that, the word "Llareggub" would be too thick and forbidding to attract American audiences. "What about *Under Milk Wood*?" he said, and I said "Fine", and the new work was christened on the spot' (*Dylan Thomas in America*, Dent 1956, p. 152). See note on 'Llareggub Hill', p. 66 below.

With the title *Under Milk Wood*, Thomas probably had in mind the way in which Laugharne (especially the lower part of the village) lies 'under' Sir John's Hill, a wooded headland on which cows graze (cf. 'at a wood's dancing hoof' in the Laugharne-based poem, 'Prologue', and 'Sir John's elmed/Hill' in the poem 'Over Sir John's hill'). If so, Sir John's Hill is what, in his own working sketch of Llareggub (opposite), Thomas named 'Llareggub Hill', with 'Salt Lake Farm' on its summit, just as the real Sir John's Hill is topped by Salt House Farm. At the same time, of course, *Under Milk Wood* wittily echoes the archetypal pastoral connotations of a phrase in Amiens' song in Shakespeare's *As You Like It* that Thomas Hardy also took as title: *Under the Greenwood Tree*.

A Play for Voices (subtitle):   Though there is no manuscript authority for using the phrase 'Play for Voices' as an actual subtitle, it does seem to have been Thomas's own phrase, certainly as recorded by John Malcolm Brinnin in this memory of summer 1951 at Laugharne: 'What he most wanted me to hear were fragments of a "kind of play for voices" he was thinking about' (*Dylan Thomas in America*, p. 103). In a letter to Marguerite Caetani in October 1951, Thomas called it 'an impression for voices' (*Collected Letters*, ed. Paul Ferris, Dent 1985, p. 813).

p. 3   ***To begin at the beginning***:   Cf. Dickens, *A Tale of Two Cities*, Bk. 2, ch. 15: 'Commence ... at the commencement' and 'All the village ... withdraws; all the village whispers by the fountain; all the village sleeps; all the village dreams ...' The very first words of *Under Milk Wood* show what is often, throughout the play, a mock-heroic humour that quotes texts more obviously serious than itself. But cf. also the opening of 'Margate – Past and Present' (1946): '1ST VOICE: Well, where do we begin? Got to begin somewhere' – a consideration repeated in another 1946 broadcast in the form of its very title: 'How to Begin a Story' (*The Broadcasts*, ed. Ralph Maud, Dent 1991, pp. 104, 122).

p. 3   ***the sloeblack, slow, black***:   The 'sloe' image, a favourite with Gerard Manley Hopkins, reminds us also of Hopkins's more general influence on the play's stylistic delight in accumulating adjectives and nouns. In this particular phrase, Thomas echoes Hopkins's fondness for paragrams (consecutive words changing only one sound or letter), e.g. Hopkins's 'How a lush-kept plush-capped sloe'.

p. 3   ***Captain Cat***:   The name raises the old idea that cats are able to see in the dark. Captain Cat, though blind, is, along with the narrator, the means whereby we 'see' a world that the voices of the characters cannot entirely reveal.

p. 3   ***the shops in mourning***:   Apart from the darkness of the night itself, the phrase evokes the 'mourning' effect of the blinds drawn overnight in shop windows. Shop blinds were also traditionally drawn during funerals.

p. 3   ***the Welfare Hall***:   Welfare Halls – a feature mainly of coalmining South Wales, established from the 1920s onwards to house 'welfare' services such as libraries, recreation rooms and clinics that had previously been left to charities to provide – were in the 1950s still an important focus of community life. The fact that they were often also Memorial Halls, dedicated to the dead of two World Wars, is part of Thomas's reference to 'widows' weeds'.

p. 3   ***jolly, rodgered***:   The Jolly Roger, the ensign of pirates, was a black flag with white skull-and-cross-bones. Thomas's punctuation also gives 'rodger' ('roger') its slang sexual meaning.

p. 4   ***Llareggub Hill***:   'Llareggub' is famous as a word that can be read backwards. Such reversible concoctions figured prominently in the compulsive word-games the young Thomas played with his Swansea friend Daniel Jones, who coined the word 'palingram' for the form. An example, in a spoof broadcast, was 'Zoilreb Pogoho will read his poem Ffeifokorp' (Daniel Jones, *My Friend Dylan Thomas*, Dent

1977, p. 24). 'Llareggub' first appeared in the early short stories of the 1930s, 'The Orchards' and 'The Holy Six'. The latter also used anagrams as the names of characters: 'Stul' (Lust), 'Edger' (Greed), 'Rafe' (Fear) etc. As it happens, among the worksheets for *Under Milk Wood* now at Texas is a note in which Thomas asks himself 'What have I missed out?' and then lists the following: 'Incest/Greed/Hate/Envy/Spite/Malice'. Nothing makes clearer the emotional distance he travelled between the raw treatment of such themes in early surrealistic short stories and their comic treatment (or omission) in the pastoral mode of *Under Milk Wood*.

p. 4　*the four-ale*:　A public house selling four types of ale. In the May 1954 première in New York, Thomas as First Voice says 'four-ale bar', obviously to help clarify the reference for an American audience (Caedmon Records TC2005).

p. 4　*with seaweed on its hooves*:　Possibly with a reference to the old tradition of padding the hooves of mules or horses drawing a funeral cart. It is the same sense of muted reverence that makes night, a few lines later, go 'gloved and folded' through the graveyard of Bethesda chapel. Cf. the 'muffle-toed tap tap', involving both funeral and mule, at the opening of the poem 'After the funeral'.

p. 4　*Bethesda*:　The names of chapels in Wales have come predominantly from place-names of the Holy Land in the Bible.

p. 4　*S.S. Kidwelly*:　'S.S.' stands for screw steamer or steamship. *Kidwelly* (an Anglicisation of the Welsh Cydweli) is an ancient Carmarthenshire seaside town, across the Towy estuary from Laugharne.

p. 4　*Davy dark*:　A reference to the sea as 'Davy Jones's [Jonah's] locker', after a sailoring name for the supposed evil spirit of the sea. But in the phrase there is also a coalmining association with the miners' safety-lamp invented by Sir Humphrey Davy (1778–1829), used in the mines from 1816 onwards. Cf. Thomas's poem 'I see the boys of summer': 'From the fair dead who flush the sea/The bright-eyed worm on Davy's lamp.'

p. 4　*the long drowned*:　Despite its maritime context, the passage in which the drowned sailors speak guiltily but longingly about their former lives shows the influence of Edgar Lee Master's *Spoon River Anthology* and of a poem such as 'Voices from Things Growing in a Churchyard' by Thomas's favourite modern poet, Thomas Hardy.

What may also have left its mark is the legend of a church and cemetery drowned by the sea in Llanina Bay, below the bungalow in New Quay that was the poet's home in 1944–45. In the 1949 broadcast 'Living in Wales', Thomas described himself as one who, 'hoofed with seaweed, did a jig on the Llanina sands'. The broadcast lists the memories that Thomas felt kept him in touch with Wales when away from home, a list that anticipates the remembered details (some vivid, others fading) that here keep the drowned mariners in touch with life: 'settles in the corners, hams on the hooks, hymns after stop-tap, tenors with leeks, the hwyl at Ebenezer, the cockles on the stalls, dressers, eisteddfodau, Welshcakes, slagheaps, funerals, and bethel-bells. What was harder to remember was what birds sounded like and said in Gower; what sort of a sound and a shape was Carmarthen Bay; how did the morning come in through the windows of Solva; what silence when night fell in the Aeron Valley' (*Broadcasts*, 204–5).

p. 5   **Nantucket**:   An island (and town) in the Atlantic, just south of Cape Cod, Massachusetts. Its Indian name means 'far away land', and its whaling associations evoke Herman Melville's *Moby Dick*, in which Captain Ahab, too, 'lost his step', in losing his leg to the whale.

p. 5   **Tom-Fred the donkeyman**:   Given the relative fewness of surnames in small communities in Wales, it became useful to identify individuals by the addition of a parent's Christian name (hence Tom-Fred), the person's job (hence donkeyman), the name of the home (Mae Rose-Cottage), or of the work-place (Mary Ann the Sailors). Several such names of people Thomas knew at New Quay, including a Dai Fred and a Mrs Evans the Lion, are mentioned by him in the letter quoted in the Introduction (p. xvii).

The term 'donkeyman' is probably not a reference to the animal, but to the 'donkey-engine', a small auxiliary engine for hauling or hoisting freight on board ship, or for pumping water into the boilers of a steamship.

p. 5   **sealawyer, born in Mumbles**:   A 'sealawyer' was an argumentative sailor always aware of his own rights, the army equivalent being a barrack-room lawyer. Mumbles is a village on the West shore of Swansea Bay, in effect a suburb of Thomas's birthplace, Swansea.

p. 6   **lavabread**:   A reflection of the Swansea pronunciation of 'laverbread' (see textual note): a dish of edible laver seaweed, traditionally associated with the area.

p. 6   **Maesgwyn**:   'Maesgwyn' (literally 'Fair Meadow') is a common Welsh name for a farm. But Thomas also had childhood memories of a farm called Maesgwyn some two miles from Fernhill, his maternal aunt's farm at Llangain, celebrated in the poem 'Fern Hill'.

p. 7   *Samson-syrup-gold-maned*:   Samson's mane occurs in the biblical story of Samson, which of course also includes a lion (Judges V, 5–9). However, the reference in this rather Joycean piece of word-play is also to the lion trade-mark for Tate and Lyle's famous 'Golden Syrup', which incorporates the sentence 'Out of the strong came forth sweetness' from the Samson story. Myfanwy Price is a 'sweetshop-keeper', and the same conjunction of ideas is picked up again on p. 29: 'MR EDWARDS [whispers]/I love Miss Price./ *Syrup is sold in the post-office*'.

p. 7   **Cloth Hall ... Emporium**:   Like the name of Mog Edwards's actual shop, Manchester House (pp. 29, 37), Cloth Hall and Emporium were typical names for drapery establishments. A Manchester House, for example, existed in both Laugharne and New Quay, the villages that influenced *Under Milk Wood*. But the satiric effect of the names also owes something to Thomas's reading of Caradoc Evans's novel *Nothing to Pay* (1930) which has a Manchester House and a Cloth Hall, as well as a catalogue of drapery wares ('flanelette' and 'calico' etc) like the one Mog Edwards recites here.

p. 7   **where the change hums on wires**:   In some large town shops (hence Mog Edwards's ambition), well beyond the Second World War, payment and change for purchased goods were sped between shop-attendant and cashier along a system of sprung pulleys and wires. Thomas would have remembered the device from the Ben Evans department store in Castle Bailey Street in Swansea, destroyed by German bombs in 1941.

p. 7   **yes, yes, yes ...**:   Evoking Molly Bloom's final, repeated 'yes' in her soliloquy at the end of James Joyce's *Ulysses*.

p. 8   *Jack Black the cobbler*:   *Under Milk Wood* is not a *roman à clef* in any strict sense. But Thomas sometimes linked name and occupation from actual memory. The following recollection by one of Thomas's very earliest schoolmates can serve as an example. It suggests that Jack Black as the name of the cobbler came from one particularly colourful memory: 'In the Uplands was a group of small shops, amongst them Mr Grey, the newsagent, Mr Black the cobbler, and White's, the shoe shop. One day, whilst a group of us waited for the school door to be opened, Dylan told us importantly that no-one was allowed to open a shop there unless their name was a colour. We all believed him, especially as, by a strange coincidence, the next shop to open was Mr Green the Greengrocer' (Joan A. Hardy, 'At "Dame" School with Dylan', *The New Welsh Review*, Spring 1995, p. 39).

p. 8   *gooseberried double bed of the wood*:   Apart from the tale that babies are found under gooseberry bushes, to 'play gooseberry' was to act as a chaperon, or to be an unwanted third presence when lovers wanted to be alone. For that sense of intrusion and exclusion, cf. 'I was alone on the gooseberry earth' in 'The Crumbs of One Man's Year' (*Broadcasts*, 154) and 'I tiptoed shy in the gooseberry wood' in the poem 'Lament'.

p. 8   *tosspots in the spit-and-sawdust*:   The habitual boozers in the cheap bars of public houses, where the only floor-covering was sawdust.

p. 8   *sixpenny hops*:   Cheap village-hall dances.

p. 8   **Ach y fi!**:   A Welsh term of disgusted disapprobation. Among the papers now at Texas, there is a note in which Thomas reminded himself to secure the correct spelling for certain Welsh words and expressions, including 'Ach y fi!'

p. 8   **making Welshcakes in the snow**:   The play is of course interested in the surrealism of dreams. For example, Gossamer Beynon, 'dreaming deep ... finds, with no surprise, a small rough ready man with a bushy tail winking in a paper carrier' (p. 14). But apart from its surrealism, the idea of 'making Welshcakes in the snow' is probably also an allusion to an old rural custom in Wales of using in the preparation of cakes and pastries, for reasons of softness and coldness as well as for other more practical reasons, water derived from melted snow. 'Welshcakes' are traditional Welsh griddle-cakes.

In an earlier version in the worksheets now at Texas the Welshcakes were originally 'fish-cakes' (then changed to 'Welshcakes'), and the dream was indoors:

> Evans the Death, the undertaker, laughs high and aloud in his sleep and curls up his toes. He knows that his mother is suddenly alive, in the kitchen, making Welshcakes, after 25 years, and he is going to climb downstairs in his little shirt and steal a fistful of currants to take up to bed and eat under the bedclothes.

p. 10   **using language**:   Using bad language. Cf. 'chalking words' (p. 11), meaning chalking naughty words.

p. 10   **Singing in the w.**:   Singing in the w.c. (water closet or lavatory).

p. 11   **Playing moochins**:   Thomas is combining the idea of 'playing dirty' (suggesting the Welsh word *mochyn* meaning pig) and 'playing truant' (for which a common Anglo-Welsh dialect word in West Wales is 'mitching'), while also suggesting to the eye the English idiom 'mooching' (loitering).

On a worksheet now at Texas, among the 'Welsh spellings wanted' Thomas included 'mwchins'. 'Moochins' turned out to be his own last choice (see Textual Notes, p. 86). In as much as it evokes the Welsh word for pig (*mochyn* – real plural *moch*), 'moochins' is illegitimately pluralised by the simple addition of an English 's'. The same thing happens in the poem 'Prologue' when the plural of *bryn* (meaning hill; real plural *bryniau*) becomes 'bryns' (cf. 'parchs', p. 17 and Note). In this way, the play reflects certain characteristics of Anglo-Welsh speech in those Anglicised areas of Wales where the Welsh language is still strong or only a generation away.

p. 11 **b.t.m.**:   That is, bottom. But the euphemistic abbreviation also plays on the name of the woman with whom Mr Waldo has been 'carrying on' – Beattie Morris.

p. 15 *Salt Lake Farm*:   There is actually a Salt House Farm on Sir John's Hill in Laugharne. Changing it to 'Salt Lake' was what gave Thomas the name 'Utah' Watkins for the farmer – after Utah, the American state of which Salt Lake City, centre of the Mormon faith, is the capital. In a worksheet now at Texas, 'Utah Watkins' was originally 'Mormon Watkins'.

p. 16 **Call me Dolores/Like they do in the stories**:   In the *New English Weekly* in November 1938 Thomas had reviewed H. G. Wells's novel *Apropos of Dolores* – the story, according to Thomas, of 'a superlatively common woman' (*Early Prose Writings*, ed. Walford Davies, Dent 1971, p. 191).

p. 17 **Eisteddfodau**:   Welsh-language competitive literary and cultural festivals. An 'eisteddfod' was originally a session or assembly of poets, the institution's name deriving from 'eistedd', meaning 'to sit'. The main modern event, the annual Royal National Eisteddfod of Wales, crowns a pattern of smaller regional and local festivals.

p. 17 *He intricately rhymes, to the music of crwth and pibgorn*:   A 'crwth' (or crowd) was a musical instrument of the lyre family, but played with a bow. It was the only instrument recognised alongside the harp by the Welsh minstrelsy in the period of the Poets of the Gentry from the late thirteenth century onwards in Wales. It remained in vogue into the eighteenth century, when it was supplanted by the fiddle. A 'pibgorn' means literally a 'horn pipe'. Though it did not enjoy the same vogue as the 'crwth' or harp in accompanying traditional, sung Welsh poetry, the 'pibgorn' also lasted well into the eighteenth century.

   The significance of the reference to the two instruments in relation to Eli Jenkins is that it portrays him as a poet capable of using the traditional strict metres of the medieval Welsh poets (hence 'He intricately rhymes ...'), as well as the less strict verses of the two poems that represent him here. Of those two, the morning poem does suggest the effects of traditional metrical intricacy, but in reality both are poems done deliberately in the manner of local newspaper verse.

p. 17 *parchs*:   'Parch' (here illegitimately pluralised by the addition of an 's') is an abbreviation and nominalisation of the Welsh adjective 'parchedig' (meaning reverend, as a religious title).

The worksheets now at Texas show Thomas clustering specific Welsh items such as 'parchs', 'eisteddfodau', 'crwth and pibgorn' for use in relation to Eli Jenkins at this stage. Two interesting items listed, but not used, were 'penillion' (literally 'verses', but specifically verses for both accompanied and unaccompanied singing) and 'Siôl Jemima' (Jemima's shawl). The latter refers to Jemima Nicholas (d. 1832) who helped defeat the French expeditionary force that landed at Strumble Head near Fishguard in 1797 by leading onto a hill a crowd of local women whose red shawls and tall hats made the Frenchmen mistake them for armed soldiers. Another idea on the same worksheet – 'Like the old wizards who made a wife out of flowers' – was employed towards the end of the play (see penultimate note below).

p. 18   **under the gippo's clothespegs**:   'Gippo' (gypsy) has to be understood in relation to 'clothespegs': well beyond the Second World War, the main objects for sale by the Romanies or gypsies travelling throughout South Wales were wooden pegs for hanging laundry on a clothesline.

p. 18   **the old man playing the harmonium in the orchard**:   In a worksheet now at Texas, this visionary picture had more pagan overtones:

> A very old God touches Mary Ann Sailors and she answers in a tongue she does not understand. She goes down those garden paths with a watering can and the old God plays his harmonium in the orchard.

p. 18   *Mrs Beynon's Billy*:   A note among the papers now at Texas shows that Thomas had thought of developing this character further:

> A new small character. Mrs Beynon's Billy, who is always faking up signs of antiquity in caves and on hills. Flints and arrows. Cave paintings. Skulls. At the end, he finds a real skull and comes screaming home.

p. 19   *The principality of the sky*:   Thomas would have been keen to bring in the word 'principality' somewhere, given its role as a word often used for Wales itself. In a note inside the back of the folder holding MS (see Textual Notes), two contending names for the street that became Coronation Street were Principality Street and Dragon Street.

p. 20   **Dear Gwalia!**:   'Gwalia', as a name for Wales as a whole, has an old-fashioned flavour that suits the character of the Reverend Eli Jenkins. Of late medieval origin, it enjoyed a remarkable sentimental revival in Victorian times, in both Welsh and English. Several nineteenth-century patriotic poems opened with an address to 'Dear Gwalia' – including, as it happens, the Welsh poem 'Cân Mewn Cystudd' ('A Song in Affliction') by Dylan Thomas's famous great-uncle William Thomas (1834–79), the Unitarian preacher, poet and Radical leader. It was from that relative's bardic name, Gwilym Marles, that Thomas derived his own middle name of Marlais, and the poet-preacher's poetic taste and populist-Unitarian persuasion may in turn have made him a vague model for Eli Jenkins himself.

Details of the Welsh mountains contrasted with Llareggub Hill are as follows: Cader Idris (Merionethshire; literally Idris's Chair [denoting a Camp], Idris being usually associated with a giant); Moel y Wyddfa (Caernarfonshire; more often Moel yr Wyddfa, literally Peak of Snowdon; the highest mountain in Wales and England); Carnedd Llewelyn (literally The Burial Cairn of Ll[y]welyn; the second highest peak in the Snowdon range); Plinlimmon (Mid Wales; an Anglicisation of Pumlumon, literally five beacons); Penmaen Mawr (Caernarfonshire, a promontory on the north coast; literally Head of Large Stone).

Carreg Cennen is a thirteenth-century castle above the Towy Valley in Carmarthenshire, 'King of time' because of its dramatic natural defences in the form of precipitous limestone cliffs.

Golden Grove is the name of a small village, and its surrounding area, in the Towy Valley, the location also of Grongar (literally Round Fortress) celebrated in John Dyer's famous pastoral poem 'Grongar Hill' (1726).

Of the eighteen rivers contrasted with the village's River Dewi, only Daw is not immediately recognisable as the name of a Welsh river. It is probably the River Ddawan (the Thaw of Aberthaw) in Glamorganshire, celebrated by Iolo Morganwg in his 'Banks of the Daw' (*Poems Lyrical and Pastoral*, 1794). Daw has also another function here. It comes at a point where Eli Jenkins's verses use an effect called 'cymeriad', characteristic of some traditional Welsh poetry, whereby words are sometimes grouped by alphabetical sequence: hence 'Claerwen, Cleddau, Dulas, Daw, /Ely, Gwili ...' Thomas's relishing of the musical effect of this traditional close patterning of consonants is clear in his rendering of Eli Jenkins's part in the original New York recording (Caedmon Records TC2005).

The equivalent of Llareggub's River Dewi in Laugharne itself is the River Corran, a narrow stream winding through the village; but it should be noted that Dewi is also the actual name of a nearby tributary of the Taf.

Though 'Taff' is simply the Anglicised form of 'Taf', it is normally used to refer to the industrial river of that name in South East Wales. It would be odd if Thomas meant that river rather than the equally alliterative 'Taf' whose estuary lay outside his window in Laugharne, and which merged with the Towy in the larger vista of Carmarthen Bay on which he looked out daily. These two local, converging rivers seem likelier subjects for the line itself – 'Taff and Towy broad and free ...' It is interesting, therefore, that it is as the Carmarthenshire 'Taf' (with a soft 'f') that Thomas can very clearly be heard pronouncing it in his reading of Eli Jenkins's part in the recording of the May 1953 première stage-reading in New York (Caedmon Records TC2005). Thomas probably thought that even the pronunciation 'Taf' (soft 'f') was spelt 'Taff'.

Eli Jenkins's recital of picturesque and dramatic place-names is in a long literary tradition, but similar listings in Edward Thomas's *Wales* (1905) seem particularly relevant, especially in their coincidence with so many of the rivers named by Eli Jenkins. About such name-lists, Edward Thomas says, 'Let me ease my memory and pamper my eyes, and possibly make a reader's brain reverberate with the sound of them' (1924 edition, pp. 15–16).

p. 24 **big-besomed**: A 'besom' is a broom. Apart from the play on big-bosomed, the 'besom' figures in several English idioms having to do with dominant or shrewish wives – e.g. 'to hang out the besom', meaning to take advantage of freedom during a wife's absence.

p. 29 **Nogood Boyo goes out in the dinghy Zanzibar**:   An earlier version among the Texas manuscripts points up the superiority of the piece as we now have it:

> I'm losing my grip, fast. The still fish flick about. He lets one foot lazy over the Zanzibar rim, and 'crunch' says the final salmon of the sea in a North Welsh voice. Foreigners have salmoned me, he says, looking at the full Swansea-seeing sea.

p. 33 **Hush, there's a hush!**:   For the lull in the gossip as Polly Garter goes by, cf. Marie Trevelyan, *Folk Lore and Folk Stories of Wales* (1909), p. 211: 'When several people talking together suddenly become silent, they said "A witch is passing". Another expression was, "Silence in the pig-market – a witch goes by" '.

p. 35 **Tallyho**:   Caitlin Thomas recalled of her father, Francis Macnamara, that 'he seemed to make love quite impersonally ... right at the crucial moment ... he would shout "Ship ahoy!" ' (Caitlin Thomas with George Tremlett, *Caitlin: Life with Dylan Thomas*, Secker and Warburg 1986, p. 14).

p. 37 **jig jig**:   A euphemism for sexual intercourse, used and understood internationally by prostitutes in sea-ports.

p. 37 **[A choir of children's voices ...]**:   When still busily seeking to finish *Under Milk Wood*, Thomas may have been confirmed in his decision to allow children's voices such a large part in the play by his visit in July 1953 to the Llangollen International Eisteddfodd in order to write a radio feature about that event. The festival's most popular success that year was the Obernkirchen Girls' Choir – which Thomas described as singing 'like pigtailed angels' (*Broadcasts*, 270).

p. 37   **(late of Twll)**:   The point about the prim proprietor Mog Edwards's previous location being 'Twll' is that *twll* in Welsh means 'a hole'.

p. 39   **'The Rustle of Spring'**:   The reference is to a salon piece of that name by Christian Sinding (1856–1941), a minor Norwegian imitator of Grieg, popular at the turn of the century. 'The Rustle of Spring' became something of a piano cliché, redolent of suburban middle-class taste. It is comically juxtaposed here with the Pythagorean idea of the 'Music of the Spheres', an allusion which in turn also brings Gustav Holst's *The Planets* suite to mind. (Cf. 'the Dance of the World', p. 59, and note.)

p. 41   **little Willy Wee**:   This name, like the form itself of Polly Garter's song, comes from nursery rhymes (e.g. 'Wee Willy Winkie'), suggesting indirectly that Polly's loss is also that of childhood. On p. 59, the Second Woman's Voice adapts an equally familiar nursery rhyme.
    It is also worth recalling that, in *Adventures in the Skin Trade* (1941), another Polly pretends to lament Sam Bennet (Thomas himself) in the same terms: 'His name was Sam and he had green eyes and brown hair. He was ever so short'.

p. 42   **It was a luvver and his lars . . .**:   The text Gossamer Beynon wants her pupils to pronounce more orthodoxly is the Pages' song from Shakespeare's *As You Like It* (V, 3), which suits the play's emphasis on springtime innocence and the passing of time.

p. 45   *cawl*:   A traditional Welsh dish, a broth of meat and vegetables.

p. 46   *salad-day*:   Cf. 'My salad days, /When I was green in judgement' (*Antony and Cleopatra*, I, 5).

p. 49   **Lord Cut-Glass**:   'Cut-glass', used of an accent, meant upper-class refined. It was a term Thomas used to describe his own un-Welsh accent.

p. 49   *a house and a life at siege*:   For Lord Cut-Glass's 'life at siege', cf. Mr Sapsea in Dickens's *Edwin Drood* (ch. 4):

> Mr. Sapsea has a bottle of port wine on a table before the fire . . . and is characteristically attended by his portrait, his eight-day clock, and his weather-glass. Characteristically, because he would uphold himself against mankind, his weather-glass against weather, and his clock against time.

p. 50   *Donkeys angelically drowse*:   The angelic demeanour of this animal was memorably celebrated in a poem read by Thomas at the Reigate

Poetry Club in October 1948 – 'Prayer to go to Paradise with the Donkeys', Vernon Watkins's translation from Francis Jammes.

p. 50   **Doctor Crippen**:   The American doctor Hawley Harvey Crippen (1862–1910), executed in London for poisoning his wife.

p. 51   **What seas did you see...**:   The poem is the heart of Thomas's own favourite part of the play. The papers now at Texas include an early shorter attempt, planned to be spoken by a 'Woman', not identified as Rosie Probert. It is interesting from the point of view of words subsequently discarded, for the way in which the original 'When you were master' confirms a naval pun in the 'When you were my master' of the present text, and for images that Thomas, in circling, thought of developing:

> *Woman*
>
> What seas did you see
> In those long whale blue sea days?
> What sea beasts were
> In the wavery green
> When you were master?
>
> Blue seas and green,
> Seas covered with fur serpents,
> And ~~walrus~~ mermaids and whale.
>
> What seas did you sail,
> Old whaler, when
> On the whiskery ~~pond~~ sea
> Between Frisco and Wales
> You were his bosun?
>
> Seas green as a bean,
> Seas gliding with deer,
> And foxes and swans.
>
> And what seas went rocking,
> My apprentice, my love,
> On your rainbowing flood?
> Cockatoos and doves
> With queens in their pockets?
>
> I am no liar.
> The only seas I saw
> Was the sea-saw sea
> With you riding on it.

p. 54   *the White Book of Llareggub*:   This is a parody of the titles traditionally given to collections of early manuscripts central to the
transmission of Welsh literature and Welsh history: for example, the
Black Book of Carmarthen, the Red Book of Hergest, the White Book
of Rhydderch etc. In an early short story, 'The Orchards' (1936), the
hero Marlais wakes from a dream 'more terrible than the stories of
the reverend madmen in the Black Book of Llareggub'.

p. 54   *a pot in a palm*:   In the original January 1954 broadcast (Argo
record RG21/22), without manuscript authority, this was changed in
Richard Burton's narration to 'a palm in a pot'. That Thomas
intended it, at least finally, as 'a pot in a palm' is shown by the Yale
TS. There, he crossed out 'pot', possibly starting to correct the phrase,
only to reinstate it again by hand. Whether the present comic touch
was originally a happy accident or not, it is highly characteristic of
Thomas's sense of satire: the palm, that cliché of front-parlour decor,
is pretentiously larger than its container.

p. 56   *glass widow*:   With an ironic play on 'grass widow' – in this context,
a wife only temporarily parted from her husband(s).

p. 56   *with tears where their eyes once were*:   Cf. Shakespeare's *The
Tempest* (I, 2, 399): 'Those are pearls that were his eyes', made newly
current by T. S. Eliot's *The Waste Land* (1922).

p. 59   *the Dance of the World*:   In both Western and Eastern literature, the
world has often been seen as coming into existence through dance and
music. (See J. M. W. Tillyard, 'The Cosmic Dance', *The Elizabethan
World Picture*, 1943, ch. 8.)
    But the 'Dance of the World' may be a bogus reference, despite its
capital letters. Its function may simply be to suggest the opposite of
the traditional Dance of Death. The actual occasion here – that of
'unmarried girls' preparing for dates at the village dance (cf. 'sixpenny
hops', p. 8) – certainly makes any esoteric allusion mock-heroic (cf.
'The Rustle of Spring', p. 39 and explanatory note), and the main
joke is that the lethargic 'drinkers in the Sailors' Arms drink to the
failure of the dance'. In poems such as 'Fern Hill', 'A Winter's Tale'
and 'In Country Sleep', Thomas celebrates analogous concepts such
as the dance of the four elements and the Music of the Spheres more
seriously.

p. 60   *that mystic tumulus, the memorial of peoples that dwelt in the region
of Llareggub before the Celts left the Land of Summer and where
the old wizards made themselves a wife out of flowers*:   Thomas
has here appropriated a particular section of Arthur Machen's *Far
Off Things* (1922), a volume later incorporated in Machen's *Auto-*

biography (1951), where the author recalls that 'as soon as I saw anything I saw Twyn Barlwm, that mystic tumulus, the memorial of the peoples that dwelt in that region before the Celts left the Land of Summer'. However, Thomas could have found the words in Gwyn Jones's *A Prospect of Wales* (1948) where the exact Machen section is quoted on page 17.

The 'Land of Summer' was the name given by the poet and antiquary Iolo Morganwg (Edward Williams, 1747–1826) to the country he claimed was the original home of the Welsh before their arrival in Britain. The name was his rendering of Deffrobani (Ceylon – thought to have been the first home of the human race) in the fourteenth century Book of Taliesin.

It seems, however, that what had captured Thomas's imagination in particular was the idea of making 'a wife out of flowers'. He entered the image on its own on several of the worksheets now at Texas, as if waiting for the right moment at which to work it into the text. It alludes to the creation of Blodeuwedd from the blossoms of the oak, the broom and the meadow-sweet, in the Welsh tale *Math, Son of Mathonwy*, the last of the Four Branches of the medieval Welsh classic, the Mabinogi. (It is from the same source that the name 'Dylan' itself derives.)

p. 60 **In Pembroke City when I was young:** Mr Waldo's song is meant to evoke the tradition of the urban broadside ballad, a nice counterpoint to other more rural songs and poems in the play, such as Eli Jenkins's morning hymn and Polly Garter's 'I loved a man whose name was Tom'.

In MS (see Textual Notes), Mr Waldo's ballad had extra lines which Thomas deleted:

> Sweep sweep chimbley sweep
> I cried through Pembroke City
> And soon a score of kind young women
> Took me in from pity
> Poor little chimbley sweep they said
> Black as a blackamoor
> Are you as nice at chimneys
> As Betty the Duckpond swore.

p. 61 **mighty Bach. Oh, Bach, fach:** The joke in calling the composer Bach 'mighty' lies in the fact that, in Welsh, the adjective 'bach' means 'small'. The final vocative 'fach' – bringing in the word's other function as a term of endearment – is incorrectly mutated on this occasion; it should be 'bach' to match the masculine subject.

TEXTUAL NOTES

TEXTUAL NOTES

The following notes indicate the differences between the present new edition of *Under Milk Wood* and the previous standard text, the J. M. Dent edition edited by Daniel Jones in 1954 and revised by him in 1974. We have used the edition reset in 1985, and we note below all the particulars where our study of the manuscripts has suggested that changes should be made.

As indicated in the Introduction the most important change is perhaps the conflation of the First and Second Voices into one voice, headed 'First Voice' at the opening of the play, with the narration thereafter distinguished from the other characters' parts typographically. This formatting device does not, of course, affect one word of what is spoken. And to communicate some sense of the poet's intention in the four places where he had the Second Voice take over in mid-sentence the narration of the First Voice, we indicate the shift by dropping the line down at that point, and noting the fact in a footnote.

The text of *Under Milk Wood* has been scrutinised by the editors in relation to the two manuscripts of the play that had, separately, what might be considered the poet's latest attention. That there are two and that they both survived, is a matter provoking some amazement. The essential story of these two copy-texts begins with the first performance of the play in New York City on 14 May 1953, the one in the Poetry Center of the Young Men's and Young Women's Hebrew Association, when Dylan Thomas himself took part and directed the play. It was tape-recorded, and subsequently issued by Caedmon Records (*Caedmon Records TC2005*). The text used by the actors in that première was typed in New York under the supervision of Elizabeth Reitell – some of it, according to her account, only minutes before curtain time:

> The curtain was going to rise at 8.40. Well, at 8.10 Dylan was locked in the backroom with me. And no end to *Under Milk Wood*. He kept saying 'I can't, I simply can't do this.' I said, 'You can, the curtain is going to go up.' Strangely enough he wrote the very end of *Under Milk Wood* then and there, and he wrote the lead-up to it. He would scribble it down, I would copy it, print it so that the secretary could read it, hand it to John Brinnin, and hand it to the secretary to do six copies. We all jumped into a cab finally, and got over to the theatre at half-past eight and handed out the six copies to the actors.[1]

[1] Elizabeth Reitell speaking on a BBC Third Programme feature (*Portrait of Dylan Thomas*, 9 November 1963), quoted in Cleverdon's *The Growth of Milk Wood*, p. 24.

This May 1953 typescript is what Thomas took back to Laugharne with him and worked on in a desultory manner for the next four months. What he did in the main was write out a fair copy of the play up to a certain point on twenty-three foolscap pages, which correspond to the first nineteen pages of the New York typescript. (These typescript pages he gave to Daniel Jones when visiting him in early October 1953 on his way to London and America again. They are now deposited in the Harry Ransom Humanities Research Center, Texas.) The rest of the May 1953 typescript, pp. 20–51, containing alterations and markings made during the New York production and for the solo reading he did at Tenby in early October 1953, was tacked on to the written-out twenty-three pages; and this is what Thomas presented to Douglas Cleverdon of the BBC at lunch-time on Thursday 15 October 1953 (Douglas Cleverdon, *The Growth of Milk Wood*, Dent 1969, p. 35). Two secretaries worked throughout the next day typing the text onto duplicating stencils in the BBC script format. Thomas wanted to collect the original on Saturday to take with him to New York on the Monday. What ensued is now part of literary anecdotage. Thomas picked up the manuscript at the BBC on the Saturday, but then lost it. Cleverdon supplied him with a copy (in fact, three copies) of what had been typed at the BBC. Thomas told Cleverdon where he might have left the original and said that, if he found it, he could have it. Cleverdon did find it, at a pub called the Helvetia, in Old Compton Street, Soho. After a court dispute with the Trustees of the Dylan Thomas Estate,[2] he sold it to the Times Book Company Ltd – but not before analysing the variants in *The Growth of Milk Wood*. This is the manuscript Cleverdon abbreviates there as 'MS', and we will follow suit. After 1969, 'MS' itself disappeared from view. The present editors were finally able to trace it to the Rosenbach Museum and Library, Philadelphia, and wish to express their appreciation for permission to quote from it.

We also have to thank the staff of the Beinecke Rare Book and Manuscript Library, Yale University Library, with respect to a photocopy of the BBC mimeographed script (here designated 'TS') which Thomas used as his working copy during the last performances of the play on the 24th and 25th of October 1953 at the Poetry Center of the Young Men's and Young Women's Hebrew Association in New York City in what turned out to be the last two weeks of his life. Elizabeth Reitell deposited the 'TS' at Yale in May 1961 along with a copy of her letter to Daniel Jones of 1 June 1954, which had accompanied a copy of 'TS' that she sent to him at that time, amply authenticating it. In this letter she explains that, though some of the markings on the pages are hers and Ruthven Todd's, '*nothing* was done, however, without Dylan's knowledge, consent and direct personal super-vision.'

The reason why the present editors have taken into consideration both

---

[2] See *Under Milk Wood: Account of an Action to Restore the Original Manuscript*, ed. J. S. Cox, The Toucan Press, Guernsey, C.I., 1969.

MS and TS is that, as the above history of the vagaries of the manuscripts should make clear, neither of the two texts is impeccable. The Yale TS, as Elizabeth Reitell's letter stresses, 'contains all changes, corrections, deletions and revisions made by Dylan up until the time of his death'. But this all happened in the hubbub of a New York performance. Even Reitell suggests that the changes made solely for the American audience should be discounted. We would go further and suggest that discrimination should be applied in respect to all the changes made during those hectic days. For instance, on p. 25 of the Yale TS we see Dylan Thomas deleting the word 'creature' in Polly Garter's lovely monologue:

> You're looking up at me now. I know what you're thinking, you poor little milky creature. You're thinking, you're no better than you should be, Polly, and that's good enough for me.

Thomas substitutes interlinearly the word 'thing' – and 'milky thing' might do, except that the next sentence is: 'Oh, isn't life a terrible thing, thank God?' The alteration of 'creature' to 'thing' must have been made in a moment of forgetfulness about that second 'thing'. We feel that, in such instances of clear loss, a last minute change cannot impose an overriding constraint on us. There is also in the Yale TS the rather drastic deletion of two now much valued passages, of which no editors – anyway, not ourselves – would want to deprive readers.

As for the Rosenbach MS, which should be authoritative in that Thomas had the leisure of Laugharne to apply himself to it, the second half of it is pretty much the May 1953 stage script, produced in circumstances no less hectic than the Yale TS. And even in the first twenty-three pages of fair copy, Thomas occasionally nodded, and produced, for instance, 'covern' for 'coven' and other small errors, which he corrected in the Yale TS.

In short, the best text of *Under Milk Wood* has to be an amalgam of the two extant sources. The Daniel Jones edition of *Under Milk Wood* (1954), especially the second edition (1974), made some good choices in the face of textual cruxes, which we are happy to follow, usually without the fuss of a footnote. The following notes, however, explain a considerable body of readings in the Jones edition with which we have had to disagree in order to present a text as definitive as can be achieved in a situation where the unfinished and complicated state of the manuscripts leaves some of the wording perforce to the judgement of editors.

Abbreviations

> **MS** = Rosenbach Library manuscript and typescript, formerly in the possession of Douglas Cleverdon of the BBC.
>
> **Yale TS or TS** = Yale Library typescript, mimeographed at the

BBC, formerly in the possession of Elizabeth Reitell of the Poetry Center, New York.

Botteghe = 'Llareggub' in *Botteghe Oscure* IX (May 1952).

Mademoiselle = 'Under Milk Wood' in *Mademoiselle* (February 1954).

p. 3   *jolly, rodgered*:   Thomas wrote 'jolly, rodgered' in MS. The BBC typist hyphenated it as 'jolly-rodgered'; but in the Yale TS Thomas restored the original form. There is no manuscript authority for the 'jollyrodgered' of the Jones edition.

p. 3   *Only your eyes are unclosed, to see*:   The BBC typist dropped the MS comma, which is here restored. There is no manuscript authority for the italicisation of 'your' in the Jones edition, nor for the running-together of this, the next sentence, and the previous sentence into one paragraph. Nor does Thomas italicise the names of the boats here, or elsewhere, as the Jones edition does.

p. 4   *hymning, in bonnet*:   The comma of the MS, omitted in the BBC typing, is restored in Thomas's pen in the Yale TS.

p. 4   *domino; in Ocky Milkman's loft*:   MS had 'dominoe' and 'lofts'. In the Yale TS Thomas deleted the 's' of 'lofts' but actually re-emphasised the 'e' of 'dominoe', a misspelling which, in agreement with the Jones edition, we have not preserved.

p. 4   *Sailors' Arms*:   The plural form with the apostrophe is Thomas's preferred spelling in MS and TS, though he is not entirely consistent throughout.

p. 4   *coms*:   The colloquial abbreviation of 'combinations' (under-clothing). Thomas had 'combs' in MS, TS and *Botteghe*, but (possibly to avoid confusion with the other sense of 'combs') in the copy of *Botteghe* used in the Institute of Contemporary Arts Reading in May 1952 he crossed it out and interlined 'coms', which we adopt.

p. 4   *seacaptain*:   One word in MS and TS, not hyphenated as in the Jones edition.

p. 4   *never such seas*:   The Second Voice took over from the First Voice at this point.

p. 4   *fish come biting out*:   In *Botteghe* these words were followed by 'like finned and lightning bugs from behind the wet green wallpaper of the undersea'. In the MS revision this became: 'like bugs from behind the wet green wallpaper of the undersea'. But then Thomas crossed it out in MS.

p. 4   ***down to his wishbone and***:   The comma after 'wishbone' in MS was deleted by Thomas in the Yale TS.

pp. 4–5   ***him*** ... / ***enjoyable*** ... / ***blisters*** ... / ***clock*** ... / ***never*** ...:   The Jones edition omits the dots of MS and TS.

p. 5   **We shared / Her name**:   The BBC mistook the capital 'W' of Thomas's MS for lower case. Thomas did not correct it in the TS. The Jones edition chose the lower case 'w', and went further, altering the 'Her' of MS & TS to 'her'.

p. 5   **sealawyer**:   Unhyphenated in MS and TS.

p. 5   **no my never**:   We follow MS here. The 'my' was altered to 'I' in the Yale TS, and 'I' appears in all printings. However, it is valuable to preserve a wording that has been attested to as Swansea dialect of the time. (Cf. the dialect 'Never should of married', p. 9.)

p. 5   **Yes, they did**:   Comma, as in MS and TS.

p. 5   **cocoanuts**:   This is Thomas's spelling in both MS and TS.

p. 6   **lavabread**:   We preserve the spelling of MS and TS as corresponding to the Swansea colloquial pronunciation of 'laverbread'.

p. 7   ***From where you are, you can hear,***:   Commas, as in MS and TS.

p. 7   ***her lover***:   Second Voice took over from First Voice at this point.

p. 7   ***barnacle-breasted flailing***:   There is no authority in MS or TS for the comma inserted after 'barnacle-breasted' in the Jones edition.

p. 7   **flannelette / cretonne**:   Thomas used 'flanellete' in MS, which was reproduced by the BBC typist and left uncorrected in the Yale TS, though another misspelling, 'cretone', was corrected by the interlining of an 'n'.

pp. 7–8   **body** ... / **roast** ... / **closed** ... / **yes** ... / ***nightmares*** ...:   The Jones edition omits the dots of MS and TS.

p. 8   ***chasing the naughty couples***:   The Second Voice took over from the First Voice at this point.

p. 8   ***bare, bold***:   Comma, as in MS and TS.

p. 8   EVANS THE DEATH: The Jones edition follows MS in giving this passage to SECOND VOICE; but in the Yale TS Thomas crossed out '2nd VOICE' and substituted 'Evans The Death', a change which we adopt.

p. 8   **goosefield**:   MS had 'goosefield', which was mistyped at the BBC as 'grassfield'. In New York Thomas, knowing that 'grassfield' was wrong, altered it to 'greenfield'. Jones preferred to follow MS, and we concur in restoring 'goosefield'.

p. 8 **Welshcakes:** Thomas's spelling in MS and TS.

p. 8 **while his mother dances:** In MS these words were followed by 'cross as two sticks'; but Thomas deleted the phrase in MS.

p. 8 *fat, pink*: Comma, as in MS and TS.

p. 8 *cold bread pudding*: Although *Botteghe* had 'cold', Thomas wrote 'old' in MS, which was typed thus at the BBC; however, the Yale TS shows that Thomas added a 'c' to restore the word 'cold'.

pp. 9–
10 **mother. / ma. / nose. / w. / poor Mrs Waldo.:** The periods in MS and TS, omitted in the Jones edition, are here restored.

p. 10 **Oh, Waldo, Waldo!:** Dots supplied in the Jones edition are not found in MS and TS.

p. 10 **Hush, love, hush. I'm widower Waldo now:** The Jones edition italicised 'widower' without manuscript authority. A rehearsal note in the margin of the Yale TS indicated that Thomas wanted this line delivered with 'more enjoyment'.

p. 11 **our mum:** The Jones edition's 'mam' (1974, not 1954) has no manuscript authority.

p. 11 **moochins:** In a worksheet now at Texas, among the 'Welsh spellings wanted', Thomas included the word 'mwchins', the spelling that appeared in *Botteghe*, and ultimately in the Jones edition. In one of the typescripts at Texas, the word was typed 'myching', which looks like an attempt to make the common Anglo-Welsh dialect word 'mitching' (i.e. *playing truant*) appear more Welsh. Thomas altered the typed word to 'muchins', possibly attempting to get closer to the sound of the word as he heard it in his youth. When he came to do the fair copy of MS, however, he wrote it as 'moochins', which he did not alter in the Yale TS, and in which he seems to be trying to incorporate also the Welsh word for pig, 'mochyn'. *Playing mochins* (i.e. playing pigs) is an expression one might well have heard in the bilingual society in which Thomas was raised. We therefore favour 'moochins', as the closest Thomas got to a Welsh dialect idiom for *playing dirty* while also combining *playing truant*. Of course, 'moochins' also serves to recall (visually but not aurally) the English idiom 'mooching' (i.e. *loitering*).

p. 12 **to be your awful:** The BBC typist capitalised the 'to' of MS, and the capitalisation was followed in the Jones edition. We restore 'to', as indicating a continuation of the Preacher's line above.

p. 12   **Mrs Ogmore-Pritchard, widow**:   The comma of MS and TS was omitted in the Jones edition.

p. 12   **who, maddened**:   MS clearly shows a period after 'who' – a mistake on Thomas's part. The BBC typist omitted punctuation, and this was followed in the Jones edition. We take it that the poet intended a comma, as he had it in *Botteghe*.

p. 13   **Oh, Mrs Ogmore! / Oh, Mrs Pritchard!**:   In MS, Thomas gave directions in parentheses to the actors. Mr Ogmore was to speak 'fearfully'; Mr Pritchard was to be 'grieving'. However, he deleted these parentheses. In the Yale TS, Thomas put notes in the margin during rehearsal: 'No sniffing' is attached to Mr Ogmore's line, and 'quicker' is attached to Mr Pritchard's.

pp. 13–   **I must blow my nose / in the woodshed**:   The BBC typist added
. 14   periods and capital letters in this passage, followed in the Jones edition. We restore the clear intention of MS that the lines should run on, punctuated only as here.

A rehearsal note on the Yale TS indicates that Thomas wanted the husbands to speak with 'more pain'.

p. 14   **in a paper carrier**:   At this point Douglas Cleverdon, in his BBC broadcast script, brought Gossamer Beynon's 'At last, my love' etc. from below to help the listening audience (*The Growth of Milk Wood*, pp. 45, 62) and this change was adopted in the Jones edition. We, however, follow MS and TS.

p. 14   **there is perturbation**:   There is no manuscript authority for the capitalised 'There' of the Jones edition.

p. 14   **P.C. Atilla Rees**:   The Jones edition altered this name to the more expected 'Attila', but Thomas (normally a very reliable speller) consistently spelled the first name as here, possibly seeking to suggest a Welsh double-'l'.

p. 15   **salt, and brown**:   MS has the comma, dropped in the BBC typing.

p. 15   **Thirty four**:   These numbers are unhyphenated in MS and TS, as also 'eighty five' on p. 23, and 'Mrs Twenty Three' on p. 33.

p. 15   **[Mrs Utah Watkins bleats.]**:   This direction to the actor is found in MS and TS. The Jones edition changed it to 'Bleating'.

p. 15   **lumps out of bed**:   Thomas gave this passage to Atilla Rees in an annotation in the Yale TS, which we follow.

p. 15   **dead to the dark, and still foghorning**:   The Jones edition leaves out the comma found in both MS and TS. Thomas wrote in the margin of MS by this passage the word 'Syntax', which implies that he was questioning its grammatical construction. However, he crossed 'Syntax' out, and retained the comma.

p. 15   **You'll be sorry for this in the morning**:   Thomas wrote a rehearsal note on the Yale TS: 'Meaner'.

p. 16   *Willy Nilly, postman*:   In the margin of this narration in the Yale TS Thomas wrote a note during rehearsal: 'Space more'.

p. 16   *Rose-Cottage*:   This name was unhyphenated in the MS, but in the Yale TS Thomas added the hyphen throughout.

p. 16   **owl meat / *springheels***:   The Jones edition has 'owlmeat' but MS and TS have it as two words, whereas MS and TS have 'springheels' as one word, not hyphenated as in the Jones edition.

p. 17   **my foxy darling**:   The lower case 'my' is in both MS and TS, indicating a run-on.

p. 17   *titbits and topsyturvies*:   In MS Second Voice takes over from First Voice from this point up until 'sea'. But in the Yale TS Thomas alters the allocation of speeches, lets First Voice continue until 'sea', and reassigns to Second Voice the passage beginning 'The owls are hunting'.

p. 17   *sea* ...:   Dots in MS and TS.

p. 17   *Belovèd*:   MS had the accent mark, which was omitted in the BBC typing.

p. 17   *parchs*:   'Parch' in Welsh is an abbreviation of the adjective 'parchedig' ('reverend') as the title of a clergyman, here illegitimately nominalised and pluralised with an English 's'. In the Yale TS Thomas deleted the word and replaced it with 'preachers', presumably for the sake of the American audience, not as a permanent change. (He omitted the whole passage in *Mademoiselle*.)

p. 17   *fast asleep*:   This was 'miles asleep' in MS; Thomas deleted 'miles' there and interlined 'fathoms', which was followed by the BBC typist and in the Jones edition. But in New York Thomas crossed out 'fathoms' and interlined 'fast', as seen in the Yale TS, a change which we adopt.

p. 17   Pssst!:   Assigning this word to Mr Pugh was another of Thomas's changes seen in the Yale TS. There is no manuscript authority for the spelling 'psst' of the Jones edition (1974).

p. 17   *Mary Ann the Sailors*:   Thomas was inconsistent in the name of this character, sometimes writing it as 'Mary Ann Sailors', which form was chosen by Jones for his edition. We choose 'Mary Ann the Sailors' throughout, without noting variants, because it is Thomas's overall preference and registers more clearly a common Welsh tradition whereby, given the paucity of surnames in Wales, a person was often identified by a nickname deriving from the individual's place of work or home. (See the Explanatory Note on 'Tom-Fred the donkeyman', p. 68.)

p. 18   **the gippo's clothespegs:**   In the Yale TS Thomas interlined above the slang word 'gippo's' the more conventional 'gypsies'' – another concession to the American audience.

p. 18   **Turkish girls. Horizontal:**   MS had 'Harems', which was followed in the BBC typing and in the Jones edition; but Thomas in New York altered the Yale TS to the wording as here.

p. 18   *An owl / And the dawn*:   The Jones edition had one paragraph here. We however adopt the three one-line paragraphs of MS and TS.

p. 18   **reverberating on.]:**   MS and TS have 'on', which is omitted in the Jones edition.

p. 18   *sleeping in the first of the dawn*:   After this in MS, following *Botteghe*, Thomas wrote: 'The hill grazes on the lower fields'; but then he deleted it, and proceeded to revise thoroughly the *Botteghe* version of the next sentence, which had been: 'and the fields go down to the hazed town, rippling like a lake, to drink'.

p. 19   VOICE OF A GUIDE-BOOK: A certain hesitancy about this speech may be indicated by Thomas's marginal 'NO', later deleted, and by the further marginal annotation 'NOT FOR NOW', again deleted. But these could have been markings indicating that the speech was to be omitted in Thomas's reading of the play in Tenby in early October 1953.

p. 19   **bylanes:**   The Jones edition added a hyphen. The MS and TS had it as one word.

p. 19   **river Dewi:**   The Jones edition has 'River', but MS and TS have lower case.

p. 19   **[A cock crows.]:**   The Yale TS indicates that the Second Voice could say these words, 'if nec'.

p. 20   *tells them, softly,*:   The Jones edition omits the commas that are found in both MS and TS.

p. 20   **Towns lovelier than ours:**   MS had 'lovlier', copied by the BBC typist; the Yale TS shows an apostrophe inserted to give 'lov'lier', which form appears in *Mademoiselle*. But *Botteghe* had 'lovelier' and we concur with Jones in accepting that emendation.

p. 20   ***Llareggub Hill / River Dewi / Heron Head***:   These 'local' names were deliberately underlined by Thomas in MS and TS. 'Milk Wood' was not, but it was italicised in the *Botteghe* printing, which we follow.

In his spelling of Welsh place-names in Eli Jenkins's verses, Thomas is inconsistent. Where the manuscripts have them in their correct (or a correct) Welsh form, we have preserved them: e.g. 'Moel y Wyddfa' (rather than Jones's 'Moel yr Wyddfa'), 'Penmaen Mawr' (rather than Jones's 'Penmaenmawr'), Senni (rather than Jones's 'Senny'), 'Dulas' (rather than Jones's 'Dulais', a different river). We have corrected Thomas's 'Llynfant' to 'Llyfnant' (where the error was akin to the metathesis that, close to Thomas's Swansea, had long since turned Dyfnant into Dynfant); 'Cerig Cennin' to 'Carreg Cennen'; 'Carnedd Llewellyn' to 'Carnedd Llewelyn'; and 'Ned' to 'Nedd', concurring with Jones in these emendations. We have not 'corrected' conventional Anglicised forms when used by Thomas himself – forms such as Dovey, Dee, Towy, etc. – again in agreement with Jones.

The seventh stanza in Eli Jenkins's poem is a conflation of two stanzas as first printed in *Botteghe*:

> By Cerig Cennin, King of time,
> *Our* ruin in the spinnet
> Where owls do wink and squirrels climb
> Is aged but half a minute
>
> By Strumble or by Dinas Head,
> Our *Heron Head* is only
> A bit of stone with seaweed spread
> Where gulls come to be lonely.

p. 21   **Oh, there's a face!**:   In revising in MS Lily Smalls's verse-like speech, Thomas inadvertently rewrote this first line without a comma after 'Oh'. The BBC typist typed the line without the comma, but, as in MS, correctly included commas after 'Oh' the four times it appears later. The Jones edition dropped all five commas, which are here restored.

After printing in *Botteghe* a version of Lily Smalls's monologue quite similar to the final published version, Thomas in MS tried expanding it. The following additional lines constitute a first and third stanza, which were subsequently thoroughly crossed out:

> There's a oil painting!
> Hair, eyes, nose, lips, everything.

> Got a moustache as well,
> There's swank!
>
> What big eyes you got!
> Big as a bluebottles
> Nice shade of custard too.
> Mind they don't drop out.

p. 21   **Cross my heart**:   Referring to this line, Thomas wrote a marginal note at rehearsal, 'Too Irish "heart" '.

p. 22   **mum ...:**   The Jones edition drops the dots after 'mum' on both occasions here, though MS and TS have them.

p. 22   **In the cat-box?:**   A rehearsal note in the margin of the Yale TS indicates that Thomas wanted this line spoken 'Slower'.

p. 22   *on the stairs:* :   The Jones edition omits the colon of MS and TS.

p. 22   **[Door creaks open]:**   The sound effect of MS and TS is omitted in the Jones edition (1974).

p. 22   **I want to see:**   The Jones edition (1974) added a period, though the MS and TS do not have it, showing that the narrator's voice that follows *states* what she sees. (See next note.)

p. 23   *Lily Smalls the treasure*:   During the New York rehearsal Thomas wrote in the margin here: 'Come in quicker'.

p. 23   *stomping out*:   The BBC mistyped the MS 'stomping' as 'stamping', which was followed in the Jones edition.

p. 23   **What for, my dear?:**   The MS 'my' was omitted in the BBC typing, followed by the Jones edition. It is here restored.

p. 23   *heavens: / observe:* :   MS and TS have colons, omitted in the Jones edition.

p. 23   **there's wives for you ...:**   Dots of MS and TS are omitted in the Jones edition.

p. 24   **high heel:**   The Jones edition hyphenates, though MS and TS do not.

p. 24   **nothing else at all on:**   The Jones edition follows MS, which does not have 'on'; but Thomas added the word interlinearly in the Yale TS.

p. 24   **homemade:**   MS and TS have this as one word; the Jones edition makes it into two words. Similarly 'lemonrind' on p. 24.

p. 24   **to my bonny new baby**:   Polly Garter's speech after these words constitutes a major revision on Thomas's part, for the *Botteghe* version continued as follows:

> and listening to the voices of the blooming birds who seem to say to me
> > CHILDREN'S VOICES (singsonging one after the other, on different notes):
> Polly / Love / Love / Polly / I love / Polly /
> Polly / Loves me / Polly / Love / Love / Polly /
> We love Polly / And Polly love / Lovely Polly /
> Loves us all ...

It is difficult to imagine how this passage would work in performance. There is evidence in Texas typescripts that Elizabeth Reitell dropped it during the retyping in New York in May 1953. Thomas noticed it was missing and wrote on the typescript: 'More "Polly" as Botteghe'. As an apparent response, there is a further note: 'I cut this, ER.' The passage was not reinstated, but a more universally satisfying monologue was composed by Thomas for Polly Garter at this point.

p. 24   **[Single long note held by Welsh male voices.]**:   MS had 'Single long high chord on strings', which was followed in the Jones edition; but in the Yale TS Thomas altered it to the wording here.

p. 24   *cats purr in the kitchens*:   MS had 'kitchen', followed in the Jones edition; but in the Yale TS Thomas added an 's'.

p. 25   **omelette**:   MS and TS have this form of the word; there is no manuscript authority for the 'omelet' of the Jones edition.

p. 26   **threw the sago**:   Thomas offered 'dumpling' as an alternative to 'sago' in the Yale TS.

p. 26   **a inch**:   The Jones edition (1974) normalises to 'an inch' the MS and TS 'a inch', which is here retained.
One of the Texas typescripts used in a New York rehearsal contained at this point Thomas's marginal note: 'With more delight'.

p. 26   **'God has come home!'**:   In the Yale TS Thomas underlines this sentence with a marginal rehearsal note: 'Give it more'.

p. 26   **Was I wounded?**:   Thomas's rehearsal note in Yale TS: 'temporary concern'.

p. 26   **'Does anybody want a fight?'**:   There is no manuscript authority for the Jones edition substituting an exclamation mark for the question mark.

p. 26   **Give us a kiss:** The 'us' was 'me' in MS, which was followed in the Jones edition; but in the Yale TS 'me' was deleted and 'us' interlined.

p. 26   **'Aberystwyth', tenor *and* bass:** The hymn title 'Aberystwyth' (Joseph Parry) found in MS and TS was changed to 'Bread of Heaven' in the Jones edition without manuscript authority. The 'and' was underlined by Thomas in the Yale TS, which we follow.

p. 26   **I *always* sing 'Aberystwyth':** One of the Texas typescripts adds the phrase 'when I'm snobbled'.

p. 26   **And then what did I do?:** After this question, the rest of the exchange between Mr and Mrs Owen is a much expanded version of the one line that ended it in the prior version: 'Then you sang Aberystwyth all over again.' This earlier line is seen in MS at the point where Thomas ended his holograph writing-out of a fair copy of the play, and began using the May 1953 typescript for the rest of the text. Against the earlier line in the typescript Thomas had written a note to himself: 'rewrite'.

p. 27   **breathed:** MS had 'snored' which was followed in the Jones edition. In the Yale TS, however, Thomas deleted 'snored' and interlined 'breathed', which we adopt.

p. 28   **It was doctored:** Above 'doctored' in the Yale TS, Thomas tried 'cured' then crossed it out and wrote 'neutered'. He was again thinking of the American audience.

p. 28   **Yesterday,:** The comma in MS and TS was omitted in the Jones edition.

p. 28   **corgis:** Thomas spelled the plural of 'corgi' (a Welsh breed of dog) as 'corgies', which was followed in the Jones edition. We have substituted the correct form.
           As shown in MS (the May 1953 typescript) Thomas was thinking of offering the American audience 'spaniels' instead, but he deleted that alternative.

p. 29   **under the dancing vests:** This was 'vests' in *Botteghe* and in the typescript used in New York in May 1953. As seen in MS, the word was there altered to 'underclothes', which appeared in the BBC typing and the Jones edition. Although Thomas did not restore 'vests' in the Yale TS, we revert to that earlier word, as the change was undoubtedly meant for the American audience only.

p. 29   **A *baby cries*:** A marginal note in Yale TS, 'Nancy cry here', indicates that Nancy Wickwire, one of the performers in New York in October 1953, was to supply the appropriate sound effect.

p. 29   **[Children's voices, up and out.]**:   Sound effects in MS and TS omitted in the Jones edition.

p. 29   *measures, with his eye, the dawdlers by, / to himself,*:   The Jones edition omits the commas of MS and TS, and hyphenates 'dawdlers by', without manuscript authority.

p. 29   *behind his eye:*:   MS had semi-colon; this was typed as a colon at the BBC; the Jones edition dropped the punctuation.

p. 29   *Milk churns*:   The hyphen of the Jones edition is not found in MS and TS.

p. 29   *short, silver*:   The Jones edition omits the comma of MS and TS.

p. 29   *He hears the voices of children and the noise of children's feet on the cobbles*:   In the Yale TS Thomas changed the sound effects as found in MS (followed in the Jones edition) to these words spoken by First Voice.

p. 30   *And the children's voices cry away*:   MS (the May 1953 typescript) had a small segment at this point, which Thomas deleted:

> (Clip-clop of horses' feet on cobbles.)
>
>   CAPTAIN CAT (loudly)
> Morning, Big Ben.
>
>   MAN'S VOICE
> Morning, Captain.
>
> (Clip-clop fades.)
> (Noise of children running on cobbles.)
>
>   CAPTAIN CAT (softly to himself)
> Glyndur Jones, late again. (loudly) You'll cop it,
> Glyndur. Put a book down your breeches.
>   (Noise of child on cobbles fades.)

p. 31   *nice clean*:   MS and TS have underlining, but the emphasis is omitted in the Jones edition.

p. 31   **and putting**:   There is no MS or TS authority for the dots before 'and', as found in the Jones edition.

p. 31   **to the kitchen,**:   The comma of MS and TS is omitted in the Jones edition.

p. 31   **How's the twins' teeth?**:   The Jones edition (1974) has 'twin's'; MS and TS have the plural 'twins''.

The following passage was in the May 1953 typescript used for MS, but was deleted:

(Noise of feet on cobbles, coming nearer.)

CAPTAIN CAT
Six, seven, eight. Plain sealed brown envelope from Liverpool for the lodger in Craig-y-Don. Don't stick a pin in it, Willy. Nine, ten, eleven, twelve, thirteen.

p. 32 **how to do in Mrs Pugh**: In the May 1953 typescript there was an added clause: 'and there's careful the lodger is getting in Craig-y-Don ...' This was crossed out in MS.

p. 32 *Down the street comes Willy Nilly. And Captain Cat hears other steps approaching*: At first, MS and TS had sound effects, as in the Jones edition, but in both MS and TS Thomas deletes the sound effects and puts them into the narration, as here.

p. 32 **an egg in it**: The 'a egg' of the Jones edition has no manuscript authority.

p. 33 *People are moving now,*: The Jones edition omits the comma of MS and TS.

p. 33 **jumper it's**: The Jones edition follows the BBC typist, who added a comma after 'jumper', where MS had none.

p. 33 **Organ Morgan's at it early**: The *Botteghe* printing (May 1952) ended at this point. Captain Cat's speeches as found there towards the end received much revision.

p. 33 **watering the town.**: There is no manuscript authority for the Jones edition's adding dots and fusing two paragraphs together that are separate in MS and TS.

p. 34 *Can you hear*: This passage is given to Captain Cat in the Jones edition without manuscript authority.
       A marginal note by Thomas to this passage asks for 'more sex'.

p. 34 *buttery foot*: MS and TS have 'foot', not the 'feet' of the Jones edition.

p. 34 [A cock crows.]: Thomas has a marginal note in MS: 'Louder'.

p. 34 [Out background organ music.]: There is no manuscript authority for the sound effects in the form ('Organ music fades into silence') given in the Jones edition.

p. 34 *shrimp nets*: The Jones edition adds a hyphen, not present in MS and TS. Just previous to 'shrimp nets' in the list, MS had 'senna pods', but it was deleted.

p. 35   **She said / Go on / Now don't you dare**:   The Jones edition uses lower case at the beginning of these lines without manuscript authority, and adds end punctuation to some of the lines in this section where MS and TS have none.

p. 36   *Outside, the sun*:   In MS Thomas has a rehearsal note in the margin: 'lighter'.

p. 36   *Evans the Death presses hard, with black gloves, on the coffin of his breast,*:   The Jones edition omits the commas of MS and TS.

pp. 36– **[Harsh] / [Tearful]**:   The Jones edition changes these to 'harshly'
37   and 'tearfully' without manuscript authority.

p. 37   *Captain Cat sea-memory*:   The Jones edition (1974) offers the emendation 'Cat's', but we follow MS and TS which are satisfactory here, with 'sea-memory' functioning adverbially.

p. 37   *where she was born,*:   The Jones edition drops the comma of MS and TS.

p. 38   **today all**:   The Jones edition adds a comma between 'today' and 'all' not in MS and TS.

p. 38   **so what is the use I say**:   After this sentence, MS (the May 1953 typescript) had: 'Butcher Beynon bought a check cap to go badgering he said'. This was deleted in MS. A note in the Yale TS (where the sentence does *not* occur) reads: 'Cut the Butcher Beynon' – which seems to indicate that some members of the cast in October 1953 were still using the May 1953 script.

p. 38   **Workhouse**:   Thomas had 'Workhouse' in MS but altered it to 'Poorhouse', presumably for the American audience in May 1953. This was typed at the BBC as 'poorhouse'. The Jones edition has 'workhouse'.

p. 38   *herring gulls heckling*:   Second Voice took over from First Voice at this point.

p. 39   **Too rough for fishing today**:   Thomas's rehearsal note on the May 1953 typescript (MS) indicates that the line should be delivered 'Lazier, Get a long'. The previous narration also had the marginal note: 'Lazier'.

p. 39   **[Keeping to the beat of the singing]**:   Stage direction as in MS and TS. The Jones edition dropped 'Keeping'.

p. 39   **[Pause.]**:   MS had 'Long Pause' (followed in the Jones edition) but the Yale TS had 'Long' crossed out.

p. 39   *tenors.*:   The Jones edition omitted the period found in MS and TS.

p. 39   *from one of her fingerbowls,*:   MS had 'the fingerbowls' but in the Yale TS Thomas changed 'the' to 'her'. Both MS and TS have the comma, omitted in the Jones edition.

p. 40   *dirty scarlet petticoat*:   MS and TS had 'yellow' (followed in the Jones edition), but Thomas in New York changed 'yellow' to 'scarlet' to conform with the colour of the petticoat earlier.

p. 40   **God is love:**   The Jones edition capitalised 'love' without textual authority.

p. 40   **That's *our* bed:**   Thomas put six exclamation marks against this line in MS, presumably as a rehearsal note in May 1953. He put five exclamation marks after 'It's Dai, it's Dai Bread!'

p. 41   **the mean old clouds!:**   At this point the MS had a sound effect followed in the Jones edition ('Pause. The children's singing fades'); but Thomas crossed it out in the Yale TS, followed here.

p. 41   **never have such loving again:**   The Yale TS has Thomas's marginal note: 'Loving not lovin''.

p. 41   **Little Willy Weazel is the man for me.:**   In MS this line was typed 'Little Willie Weazel was the man for me' both times it occurs, but in the second occurrence (that is, the last line of the song) the 'was' was crossed out and 'is' interlined, and this was followed by the BBC typist. That typist typed the twelfth line as 'Little Willie Wee was the man for me'; Thomas altered this in the Yale TS by crossing out 'Wee was' and interlining 'Weazel is'.

p. 41   *the town, to*:   The Jones edition lacks the comma of MS and TS.

p. 42   *Love, sings the Spring*:   In the margin of MS here Thomas wrote: 'more singing'.
         Here the Jones edition omits a passage of about eleven lines down to 'says Sinbad Sailors', which Thomas had crossed out in MS as not to be read in Tenby. The BBC typist skipped over them, but Thomas replaced them in New York in the Yale TS, presumably from a copy of the May 1953 script retained by Elizabeth Reitell.

p. 42   *answers,*:   Comma as in MS and TS, dropped in the Jones edition.

p. 43   CHILDREN'S VOICES: The changes to these two lines made in the Jones edition have no manuscript authority.

p. 43   **Ding:**   The Jones edition uses lower case instead of the capital letter of MS and TS.

p. 43   *cobbles* ...:   The dots of MS and TS are left out of the Jones edition.

p. 44   **I kiss you in Goosegog Lane:**   The Jones edition ends the line with a period not found in MS and TS.

p. 44   **penny, mister:**   The Jones edition drops the comma of MS and TS.

p. 44   **Kiss me in Milk Wood:**   In MS Thomas wrote in the margin of this line 'a bird in a bush', and then deleted it.

p. 45   **said I mustn't:**   As in MS. The BBC typist typed 'says', which was followed in the Jones edition.

p. 45   *barefoot women:*   In MS the women were also 'knickerless', but Thomas deleted that word.

p. 45   *cawl:*   MS and TS have 'cowl'. A Texas typescript has 'cawl' altered in Thomas's hand to 'cowl'. As in the Jones edition, we print 'cawl', the Welsh word for a particular kind of broth.

p. 46   *nugget / coughdrops:*   The Jones edition hyphenated 'coughdrops' and emended 'nugget' to 'nougat' without manuscript authority.
    From the typed list in MS Thomas deleted: 'humbugs', 'a hot pennorth of brandyballs', 'tooth-loosening toffee of tar' and 'stale bags of black boiled marbles'.

p. 46   *street steaming / cockcrow:*   These forms are as in MS and TS.

p. 46   *she tells the stripped and mother-of-the-world big-beamed and Eve-hipped spring of herself:*   MS has marginal word: 'more'.

p. 46   *forever:*   MS and TS have 'forever', which we follow. The Jones edition has 'for ever'.

p. 46   *He grieves to his Guinness.:*   MS and TS have 'He', not the 'he' of the Jones edition. We have followed the Jones edition in supplying the correct trade name for Guinness, which Thomas spells 'guiness' in MS and TS.

p. 46   **Gossamer B.,:**   The Jones edition lacks the period, as found in MS and TS.

p. 47   *she turns, in a terror of delight,:*   The Jones edition omits the commas found in MS and TS, but adds a comma after 'conflagration' not in MS and TS.

p. 47   *toxologists:*   We have preserved Thomas's attractive neologism as found in MS and TS, for which the Jones edition gives the more correct 'toxicologists'.

p. 48   *dining vault*:   Not hyphenated in MS and TS.

p. 48   **in Milk Wood**:   These words were crossed out in MS, and omitted in the BBC typing, but they were reinstated in the Yale TS.

p. 48   **Oh, they didn't fool me**:   MS has this underlined, with a May 1953 rehearsal note: 'more', later deleted.

p. 48   **Tom Spit**:   The original MS 'Tom' was changed to 'Bob', which appeared therefore in the BBC typing (and in the Jones edition); but Thomas altered it back to 'Tom' in the Yale TS.

p. 48   **Oh, Bach without any doubt**:   MS has Thomas's rehearsal note in margin: 'more'.

p. 49   *– (one for each year of his loony age) –*:   The Jones edition changed to commas the parentheses and dashes of MS and TS, which we restore.

p. 49   *heart-knocks / chime and tock / tick tock*:   These are the forms found in MS and TS, emended in the Jones edition.

p. 49   *pretty Polly hums and longs*:   MS has Thomas's rehearsal note from May 1953: '(parenth[es]is casually)'.

p. 50   **arms –**:   The dash of MS and TS is dropped in the Jones edition.

p. 50   **[A long silence.]**:   Thomas added 'long' in the Yale TS.

p. 50   *Pigs grunt*:   MS had 'a pride of pigs grunts'; but Thomas wrote 'No!' in the margin and later altered it.

p. 50   *He puts on a soft-soaping smile*:   MS had 'He tries to put on'; Thomas deleted 'tries to' and added an 's' to 'put'. In the Yale TS Thomas has a rehearsal note: 'No "tries"' – which again implies that the actor was using a May 1953 script.

p. 50   *prussic circle of cauldrons*:   Thomas marked this passage in the Yale TS and wrote a rehearsal note: 'quicker more staccato'.

p. 51   *with a wheedle*:   After these words in MS came: 'and down the coiled stairways of her ear seethes boiling hemlock and oil' – subsequently deleted.

p. 51   *Captain Cat, at his window*:   MS shows that this passage was much revised in three successive stages from the original typed passage, which was as follows:

Captain Cat, at his wide window, slumbers and voyages, tatooed and ear-ringed and rolling on the old clippered seas, brawls with broken bottles in the fug and babel of the dark dock bars, has a herd of short and good-time-cows in every naughty port, tatooed with Union Jacks and little women who hula shimmy and ripple and I love you Rosie Probert on his belly he roves those dead sea days and the drowned and cut-throat hair-dyed high breasted schooner-and-harbour-town dead go with him dancing and slashing and making ghosts' love; and the tears run down his grogblossomed nose.

p. 51   *blowsy-breasted*:   There is no manuscript authority for the Jones edition's 'blowzy-breasted'. The MS had 'blowsy-breasted', which was typed at the BBC as 'blousy-breasted'. Thomas's spelling probably sought to fuse 'blowzy' and 'blouse'.

p. 51   *and the tears run down his grog-blossomed nose*:   This phrase was in the May 1953 typescript, but was inadvertently left out when Thomas revised MS and thus was not included in the BBC typing (or in the Jones edition). However, Thomas wrote it in on the Yale TS.

p. 51   *from the bedroom of her dust*:   Thomas tried inserting 'short-time' before bedroom, but then deleted it.

p. 51   *Mrs Probert – / Rosie –*:   Thomas added pencil dashes to the MS, which were typed in at the BBC. The Jones edition substituted dots. MS and TS also had 'From' capitalised, rather than the Jones edition's lower case.

p. 52   **sugar sailor**:   There is no manuscript authority for the period at the end of this line in the Jones edition. Thomas had marginal lines against this passage in MS (the May 1953 typescript) with the word, 'more'.

p. 52   **Rosie Probert**:   In MS Thomas added the word 'repetition' in the margin of this line of Captain Cat's.

p. 53   **crying. / *crying,* / Come back come back/nose...**:   The Jones edition emends the punctuation of this passage without manuscript authority.

p. 54   *lies silky, tingling uneasy*:   Commas are added in the Jones edition without manuscript authority.

p. 54   *grass, ho ho*:   The comma of MS and TS was left out in the Jones edition. MS had 'sweet in the grass you liar', which was deleted and the present words interlined.

p. 54   *Lifework: / worships in:*:   The Jones edition substituted dashes for the colons of MS and TS.

p. 54   *blackcloth diningtable*:   MS 'blackcloth' was mistyped at the BBC as 'black-clothed' (followed in the Jones edition). MS and TS have 'diningtable' as one word, not hyphenated as in the Jones edition.

p. 54   *in her stays*:   MS had the additional words 'and smiles', but they were deleted.

p. 55   **Oh, angels be careful there with your knives and forks**:   The comma of MS and TS was left out in the Jones edition. This line had been part of the narration in MS but Thomas reassigned it to the Rev. Eli Jenkins there. The Yale TS shows it as deleted.
         A few lines earlier, in the Yale TS Thomas also deleted the following words: 'next to faint lady watercolours of pale green Milk Wood like a lettuce salad dying'. Both were omitted in the *Mademoiselle* printing. We ignore these deletions.

p. 55   *grieved*:   Past tense in MS and TS. The Jones edition changed it to the present tense.

p. 55   *licks his hand*:   MS had 'hand', which was mistyped at the BBC as 'hands' (followed in the Jones edition).

p. 55   *he raves-and-dances*:   MS had hyphens, which were dropped by the BBC typist and also omitted in the Jones edition.

p. 55   *summerbreath'd*:   MS has 'summerbreathed' (followed in the Jones edition), but in the Yale TS Thomas deliberately crossed out the 'e' and substituted an apostrophe to secure the desired meaning.

p. 55   *They bow their heads*:   In MS Thomas wrote 'Holy' against this line, then deleted it.

p. 56   *love-light* / cripple! – / *dusk-shower* / *Sea View* / *high-backed*:   These are the forms found in MS, and adopted here.

p. 56   **Husbands**:   This exchange, down to 'take them off', was deleted in the Yale TS and did not appear in *Mademoiselle*. We ignore this deletion.

p. 57   *listening to the nannygoats*:   MS had 'and listening', which was changed in the BBC typing to 'listens', which appears in the Jones edition; but Thomas crossed out 'and' in the Yale TS and interlined 'listening'.

p. 57   *And at the doorway*:   MS has 'The Reverend Eli Jenkins's Sunset Poem' on two separate small sheets headed A and B with a note in the typed pages 'Insert A and B'. Two of the deleted lines of A are:

         Look mercifully down, I pray,
         And let us love thee in our way.

p. 57   **Every morning, when:**   The comma of MS was dropped in the BBC typing, which was followed in the Jones edition.

p. 58   **Bless us this holy night, I pray,:**   MS (sheet 8) had 'this holy night'; 'long dark' was interlined, then deleted; then 'winding' was interlined. In writing out the verse afresh, Thomas wrote 'winding' but then deleted it with no word to replace it, so no adjective appeared in the BBC typing. In the Yale TS Thomas interlined 'holy'. There is no manuscript authority for 'Bless us all this night' of the Jones edition (1974).

p. 58   **And say goodbye:**   MS had 'And say, Goodbye'; this was typed at the BBC as 'And say, goodbye'; then Thomas crossed out the comma in the Yale TS, which we follow.

p. 58   *Cherry Owen, sober as Sunday*:   This line began with 'And' in the MS and was so typed at the BBC; but Thomas crossed out the word in the Yale TS.

p. 58   **And aren't I a lucky woman? Because I love them both:**   MS has Thomas's rehearsal note: 'slower'.

p. 59   **The *Sailors'* Arms is always open, / Oh, Gossamer:**   The BBC typed MS '*Sailors*' without underlining, and the italics are also missing in the Jones edition.
     There is no textual authority for the dots of the Jones edition, or for its lower case 'oh'.

p. 59   **Oh, Gossamer, open yours!:**   From here down to Mr Waldo's song was written and added in New York in October 1953.

p. 59   *waves, / wind blows, / bough breaks,*:   These are the forms and punctuation of TS, changed in the Jones edition without manuscript authority.

p. 59   **[Accordion music:**   Sound effects in TS are as here.

p. 59   FIRST DRINKER / SECOND DRINKER: There is no authority for the Jones edition's assigning these lines to 'A Drinker' and 'Cherry Owen'.

p. 60   *Llareggub Hill, writes the Reverend Jenkins*:   There is no textual authority for assigning this passage to Eli Jenkins, as the Jones edition did, nor for the device of repeating 'Llareggub Hill'.

p. 60   **chimbley sweep:**   There is no manuscript authority for the hyphen of the Jones edition.

p. 60   **Black as the ace of spades:**   As seen in the holograph notebook page marked 'C' included in MS, this line, in what is there called 'Mr Waldo's Song', was

> Black as a Blackamoor

which rhymed with the original line-but-one after it:

> Since my husband went to war.

Thomas interlined the new wording for these lines, as adopted here. This song was called 'Mr Waldo's Pub Song' in a Texas TS.

MS had no punctuation except for the final exclamation mark and had a stanza break before the six-line refrain starting 'Come and sweep my chimbley'. The BBC typescript had no stanza break and provided punctuation, followed by Daniel Jones. We follow MS in regard to no punctuation and to separating the refrain. We have also chosen to mark with stanza-breaks the quatrain rhyme-scheme of what is essentially a ballad form.

p. 60   **Oh nobody's swept:**   'Oh', as in MS and TS, not the 'O' of the Jones edition.

p. 61   *the voyages of his tears,*:   The Jones edition omits the comma found in MS and TS.

p. 61   *Curly Bevan's skull*:   We follow MS and TS in assigning this line to the narrator rather than, as the Jones edition does, to First Drowned.

p. 61   *He plays alone at night to anyone who will listen: lovers, revellers, the silent dead, tramps or sheep.*:   This sentence is inserted in the Yale TS, not in Thomas's hand, but, we assume, on Thomas's authority. Roughly the same sentence is found in a Thomas list in the worksheets now at Texas, in which he gives thumb-nail sketches of various characters in the play.

p. 61   **Who?:**   In the Yale TS Thomas added a marginal rehearsal note: 'Drunker'.

p. 61   **Bach, fach:**   The Jones edition omits the comma found in MS and TS.

p. 61   *sea-end*:   Hyphenated in MS and TS, but not in the Jones edition

p. 62   **for ever:**   MS and TS had 'forever'; we accept the emendation 'for ever' of the Jones edition.

p. 62   *drunk in Milk Wood*:   MS had 'drunk in the dusky wood'; it was typed so at the BBC and was followed in the Jones edition, but Thomas changed it to 'Milk Wood' in the Yale TS.

p. 62   *But it is* **not** *his* **name**:   In the Yale TS Thomas added a marginal rehearsal note: 'softer'.

p. 62   *Mary Ann the Sailors who knows there is Heaven*:   The name in
MS and TS is as here, and there is no manuscript authority for the
'a' of the Jones edition before 'Heaven'.

p. 62   *bridebeds*:   MS 'bridebeds' was typed at the BBC as 'bridesbeds',
which was followed in the Jones edition.

ACKNOWLEDGEMENTS

The editors wish to thank the Beinecke Rare Book and Manuscript Library of Yale University Library; The Bodleian Library, Oxford; the Department of Manuscripts of the British Library; the Harry Ransom Humanities Research Center of the University of Texas; the Rosenbach Museum and Library, Philadelphia; and the libraries of Simon Fraser University, British Columbia, and of the University of Wales, Aberystwyth.

Thanks are also due to the following individuals who helped with encouragement or practical assistance at various turns: Paul Ferris, Malcolm Gerratt, Cathy Henderson and Hilary Laurie.

Grateful acknowledgements are extended to the British Academy and the Social Sciences and Humanities Research Council of Canada for grants awarded for research work on both sides of the Atlantic.